soap making
naturally

dedicated to Jonas Mahloko, my dear and precious
soap maker who died of stomach cancer in 2008

0 11557 01771 7

soap making
naturally

bev missing.

STACKPOLE
BOOKS

contents

introduction

Never in my wildest dreams did I think I would be writing a book. It has been on my to-do list for over 30 years, but more because it sounded grand and aspirational than because it was something I thought I could actually achieve. When Wilsia Metz invited me to do this book, I was both excited and terrified. What if I failed? I have shops that sell soaps, and I earn my livelihood from the sales of soaps – how could I share all my trade secrets with people who might become my competition in the marketplace?

I was invited not because of my literary skills, but because I have taken a hobby and made it into an international brand, and this alone gave me a modicum of credibility to be invited to share my trade secrets and my company's journey with aspiring crafters. I have invested an enormous amount of intellectual property into the formation of my company, RAIN. It started in the days before YouTube and Google and when we only had very slow limited dial-up internet access in rural South Africa – so surfing the web was impossible. I had no mentor, no one to teach me, no access to courses, special ingredients, moulds, colours. I only had a few library books to guide me.

Formulating my natural soaps took two years of struggle. I bought every book I could find on soap making, only to find the recipes did not work, or I could not source the ingredients. It was a highly secretive closed industry and as I was living in a tiny village, I was stuck. One day, in desperation, I searched on the very slow, unreliable internet in the hope of finding some information that might help me. I found myself in a chat room, so I sent a message into the great blue yonder and asked if anyone in the world could help me to make soap.

Well, believe it or not, I got a reply! From a lady in the far USA called Therese Lott. She was like an angel sent from heaven. I imagined her broad American accent as she wrote her emails to me, asking which oils I could find in my area. I replied, and she promised to have her friend over for a few days and to make up a few recipes for me to try. She was faithful to her promise, and a week later, I received a few soap recipes to try. Therese then mentored me over a two-year period while I experimented (I had a full-time job running a 26-roomed guesthouse and restaurant, so it took time!). Had it not been for this kind, generous, open-hearted lady and her unnamed friend, my brand, RAIN, might not have been born.

After two years of practice and experimentation, determined to make an excellent all-natural product, I felt confident enough to launch it on an official trade show – available to retailers to stock in their stores. It just took off. The RAIN brand was born. I was inundated with orders and my little business grew from strength to strength, becoming a fully fledged stand-alone international body and bath product brand with retail stores in South Africa, Amsterdam and New York.

Africa is a continent of poverty that can only be alleviated by creating work and income, and my vision for the company was to create job opportunities for the locally unemployed. In August 2012, after 13 years of operation, we achieved our international Fair Trade status as a brand – something that makes me immensely proud. We plan to open very special limited stores worldwide and to keep our ethic of intensely handmade and natural, with a core mission of creating hope, teaching skills and making a difference in our little town of Swellendam, South Africa.

So, to be totally honest, having struggled so hard to learn to make soaps and from there to build my own brand, it took a real mind shift for me to decide to share openly in this book my journey and my secrets. I believe in reaping what you sow and in paying it forward. Therese generously helped me all those years ago, so I owe a debt to help others too. Hence this book.

I would like to invite you to follow the highs and lows of the incredible RAIN journey. Read the stories about the amazing people who make RAIN products near the southernmost tip of Africa on my **personal blog** rainqueendoodles.blogspot.com. This is where where I share the personal side of my work and tell stories about journeys to find special and unique ingredients, as well as the special people I meet along the way. On **YouTube**, RainAfrica is our very own channel where you can watch video tutorials demonstrating the step-by-step and how-to side of this book. Access these at www.rainafrica.com/tutorials.

You will also find more information on our **website** (www.rainafrica.com). On **Facebook**: Rain – created for living (South Africa); Rain Africa (USA); Rain Africa – Nederland (Europe). On **Twitter**: @rain_africa; @bevmissing. On **Pinterest**: RAIN – Bev Missing.

Finally, I would like to appeal to you to honour the intellectual property I am sharing in this book, to use it wisely and to remember that it should be passed forward to benefit others and not be selfishly and greedily held onto. Formulate your own unique recipes and designs if you are going to become a commercial soap maker.

(1)

equipment you will need

The good news is that you probably already have everything you will need in your kitchen. What is more, you can use various items for making both food and soap, the only caveat being that you wash everything thoroughly with vinegar water after making soap (use 1 cup of white vinegar per sinkful of soap-making equipment).

Over time, wooden items will become damaged from exposure to highly alkaline or caustic solutions, so you may want to keep a set of these exclusively for soap making.

Soap causes aluminium to corrode, so avoid aluminium pots, moulds, drying pans and utensils. Also avoid cast iron and Teflon. Stainless steel is the material of choice, and enamel also works well.

Moulds can be made of silicone rubber, plastic or wood. Silicone moulds are easier to work with as the flexibility of the silicone allows for easy release of the soaps. With wooden moulds, you have to use paper mould liners to enable you to get the soap out of the mould. The best wooden moulds are ones with piano hinges and drop-down sides. These can very easily be made in your garage. Silicone moulds are costly and, if you plan to make soaps commercially, you will need many – so bear this in mind when choosing a shape.

Essential safety items

- Safety goggles (hardware store)
- Mask (pharmacy)
- Surgical gloves (pharmacy)

Other essential equipment

- Plastic/rubber spatulas (kitchen shop)
- Glass thermometer (baking shop or pharmacy)
- Sturdy plastic jugs
- Pyrex or microwaveable glass measuring jug with capacity of at least a quart (a liter)
- Stainless steel pots, large and small – the recipes in this book call for a 4-quart (4-liter) pot, but should you wish to upscale, invest in a 12-15-quart (12-15-liter) pot
- Old blanket, sleeping bag or towels – they will get messy
- Electronic scale, 0-11 lb (0-5 kg), with a tare function
- Electric stick blender
- Silicone moulds (baking shop)
- Wooden moulds – make your own (I have not found them in any stores), or order online at www.brambleberry.com
- Other moulds (see note opposite)
- Wooden or stainless steel stirring spoons – not to be used for food
- Stainless steel measuring spoons
- Cloths or paper towels
- Muslin or cheesecloth and sieve, for straining lumps out of colours and additives
- Plastic covering to protect work surface
- One or two sturdy plastic 5-quart (5-liter) buckets for your lye solution
- Hot plate or stove top
- Cheese grater
- Masking tape
- Packaging tape
- Heavy-duty wax paper, parchment paper or plastic wrap to line wooden moulds
- Large non-serrated knife to cut the soaps
- Small, thin non-serrated paring knife to trim the soaps
- Ruler
- Plastic teaspoons and small plastic bowls for blending colourants and preparing additives – at least 4–6
- Calculator
- Drying rack or cardboard beer trays from the bottle store
- Plastic or wooden cutting board
- Plastic wrap and/or cellophane for wrapping finished soaps

Nice-to-have items

- Small stainless steel whisk or electric milk frother to blend your colours and remove the lumps
- Specialised moulds from international soap-making suppliers
- Dedicated drying shelves
- pH test strips
- Airtight glass bottles for storing your colours
- Paper labels for above
- Piping bag and nozzles
- Plastic pipettes
- A wooden mould with silicone lining and Perspex dividers (from online shops only)
- A fabulous customised soap cutter (see suppliers section)
- Coffee grinder or pestle and mortar to powder and grind spices, herbs, etc.

A NOTE ABOUT MOULDS

Moulds can really make a difference to your soaps. It has always been a challenge to find decent moulds, but recently some fabulous silicone baking moulds and cupcake or muffin pans have become available in kitchen shops and supermarkets. These are ideal.

You can make your own wooden loaf moulds with piano hinges to enable the sides to fold down for easy extraction of the soap. These are dead easy to knock together.

You can make temporary shapes from cardboard cereal boxes taped together, from plastic bottles cut down, from Pringles tubes, or from PVC drain pipes (square or round).

I am always looking out for possible moulds, which can be found in surprising places such as food markets, kitchen shops or shops selling items like car spares, plastic storage containers or rubber fittings. You can even use muffin packaging. Don't discard any packaging before considering its possible use as a soap mould.

PREPARING MOULDS

- Silicone moulds need no preparation whatsoever – that is the beauty of them – they are ready to pour and go.
- Wooden moulds need to be lined with plastic wrap or parchment paper – fold neatly and carefully to minimise creases and lines which will show on your pre-trimmed soap.
- Metal and plastic moulds can be used without preparation, but the soap will not easily release and you may need to freeze them to get the soap to contract enough to get it out.

ingredients

As a crafter, you can follow the project recipes, but if you are hungry for knowledge and want to create your own formulas, a deeper understanding of the various ingredients and how they function is essential. Don't panic about the chemistry – I have simplified everything to make it easy to understand. To play with the projects later in the book, you only need to master one basic recipe described under Step-by-step cold-process soap making (see page 75).

oils and butters/fats

Oils and butters are the heart of your soap and how you choose and combine them is crucial to the end product. Oils and butters or fats are different only in that one is a liquid at room temperature and one is a solid. Usually fats are animal products, butters are derived from plants, vegetables or nuts, and oils are vegetable, but not always. Some oils are artificially induced to stay solid at room temperature – like margarine. This is done through a process of hydrogenation, which means the oils are pumped with hydrogen to change their molecular structure. I never use any hydrogenated fats in cooking or in soap making. I see them as artificial, foreign and harmful, with warped molecular structures that can only be bad for my body!

There are many different types of oils and fats and virtually all of them have the ability to saponify. They all have unique properties based on their molecular structure (their fatty acid chains), so the art and science of soap making rests in the careful selection and combination of various oils, bringing each one's properties, benefits and features to the soap party – some bring hardness of bar, some bring lathering ability, some hold the lather in place once it is formed, some bring great moisturising properties, some bring slip and glide, and some bring various antioxidants, vitamins and omegas.

You may also choose an oil or fat because it's easy to source, affordable or because it's grown and produced near you, offering a low carbon footprint, clear environmental sustainability and benefits to local communities.

The oils we use at RAIN have been carefully researched to bring the best skin-nourishing properties, but also purchased with a Fair Trade conscience and ethic. We use wild harvested African oils, not only because they are organic, pesticide and fertiliser free, but because they support impoverished communities and are harvested from wild trees by women who earn their livelihood from selling these oil-bearing seeds. Our base oils also come from farms near our factory.

Sadly, we don't have palm oil in South Africa, but we source our palm oil from a hundred-year-old plantation in Malaysia, where firm environmental policies are in place and where the farmers are founder members of the Round Table on Sustainable Palm Oil Production (RSPO), an organisation devoted to sustainable palm oil production and actively involved in the rehabilitation of endangered species, especially orangutans. Plantations such as these provide much-needed employment opportunities in a very poor region. So there is always the flip side of the coin to consider when making a purchase.

Research your sources and make sure you are buying wisely and supporting global ethics.

sunflower   flaxseed   coconut   rosehip   grapeseed   macadamia
                                                                            nut

Below is a list of the most commonly used oils in soap making. There are many others. In order to be able to use an oil in your soap formula, you will need to find out its SAP value. Use the Saponification chart on page 167, or ask the oil supplier for a material safety data sheet. SAP values can vary according to the regions where the oils are harvested and their fatty acid contents, but I have included enough detail for you to be able to make excellent soap. If your chosen oil is not on the chart, it doesn't mean it can't be used. Research its saponification value for both sodium hydroxide and potassium hydroxide, so that you can use it for both solid and liquid soap making.

I have stated the suggested use for each oil in one of three categories:

Core oil – forming a large portion of your formula
Supplementary oil – forming a small portion of your formula
Superfatting – used as an additive

tip: Soap can be made using only one fat or oil, but inevitably the soap may lack certain qualities – for example delivering a good frothy fluffy lather, or be soft and sticky, or be drying to your skin.

| apricot kernel | avocado | castor | pomace olive | wheat germ | extra virgin olive |

SUPERFATTING

When you use a lye calculator to formulate the amount of lye and water required to turn your oils and fats into soap (to saponify them), you will be given a weight of lye and a weight of water for your recipe. Your end soap will then be fully and completely saponified, which means it will not contain any excess oils.

Superfatting is where you don't allow for the weight of a particular oil when you calculate how much lye you will need. It is added in a small quantity – usually around 3 to 4 tsp (15 to 20 ml) per 2.2 lbs (1 kg) of oils – at trace when the lye is at its least aggressive, thereby preserving the oil's properties and technically allowing it to remain in the soap as an unsaponified oil. This is done to carry its properties through to the end soap and also to make it extra creamy and moisturising. It gives you a much milder soap, as it cleans but does not strip the skin of its protective hydrophobic film barrier.

The chosen ingredient for superfatting should be melted before adding and cooled to room temperature 75.2°F (24°C) when you add it at trace together with the fragrance oils.

You can also superfat the soap by taking a 5% lye discount (using less lye than you ought) on the lye calculator for the initial formula, rather than adding the extra fats at the end. This means you have 5% less lye particles to marry with your oil particles during saponification, leaving some of them floating around unattached and thereby adding creaminess and moisture to your bar – a fully saponified bar could be on the harsh side. The secret to a rich, creamy, mild soap that cleans without drying the skin is to test the limits of lye discount. Trial and error shows that a discount of 5–10% is workable. Err on the side of a lesser discount if using oils with a short shelf life, or if using oats and other grains in your recipe. For oils with really short shelf lives, like hemp seed, I choose not to take any discount at all.

You can also choose to do both – take a 2–5% lye discount (which I always do) as well as superfat at trace – as long as you don't exceed an overall total of 6–8% discount. Remember that this will affect the shelf life of your soaps, as the unsaponified oils, while delivering a superbly rich bar, will also eventually turn rancid and begin to smell like stale oil, and show brownish-orange spots. Fully saponified soaps can last for decades, but superfatted soap only a year or three, depending on the oils used and degree of superfatting.

MOST COMMONLY USED OILS

Coconut oil

INCI name: Cocos nucifera

SUGGESTED USE:
Core oil – use at 20–30% of the formula.

The coconut palm produces oil pressed from the dried flesh of coconuts – the copra – and this is one of the core oils in soap making. No more than one-third of your formula should consist of coconut oil, or it will be quite drying to the skin. (Yes, coconut oil is an anomaly – a little moisturises and too much dries!) It can typically be found at speciality delicatessen stores, Asian supermarkets, wholesale bakery suppliers and even pharmacies although the latter at a premium price. It comes in various types:

- **Virgin** – this is similar in fatty acid profile to the other versions of coconut oil, but it comes from the pressing of the wet coconut flesh rather than from the dry flesh. This may or may not use heat – if not, it is cold pressed. It has a real coconut smell and taste.
- **Fractionated** – a fraction of the coconut oil in which the long-chain triglycerides are removed, resulting in an oil with a longer shelf life and higher relative concentrations of capric acid and caprylic acid, making it lighter and more effective as an antioxidant and a disinfectant. Its lightness makes it more easily absorbed into skin and hair without adding heaviness, and the deeper penetration means it moisturises more deeply. Commercial companies use this version of coconut oil to make a claim that the product is oil free. It has its own INCI name: Caprylic/ Capric triglyceride.
- **Organic** – no pesticides and chemicals are used in the growing of the coconuts.
- **Cold pressed** – the oil is extracted without the use of heat, thereby preserving the properties of the oil. It's usually quite expensive.
- **Refined** – the oil has been bleached and deodorised and the taste and smell of coconut is no longer present.

Different melt points – 75.2°F (24°C), 91.4°F (33°C), 109.4°F (43°C). The one you're most likely to find is the 75.2°F (24°C) version. All are acceptable.

SOAP-MAKING QUALITIES

- Low-cost oil
- Good fluffy lather, even in cold water
- Quick to lather
- Whiteness of finished soap
- Good cleansing ability
- Adds excellent hardness to the bar
- Very long shelf life of 2–4 years if stored properly
- Easy to source
- Highly stable oil
- Traces quickly
- Highly saturated, so soap does not quickly become rancid
- Use in combination with highly emollient oils to compensate for drying effect
- Strong odour, but odour does not follow through into the end soap

EFFECTS ON SKIN

- Moisturising, but becomes drying in high doses
- Helps repair sun damage
- Antibacterial
- Good for hair follicle penetration in shampoos and conditioners
- Aids skin elasticity
- Its lauric acid content is antibacterial
- Contains ferulic acid, which is a powerful antioxidant and reduces signs of ageing
- Reduces itching and inflammation, but it can clog pores and should not be used for acne
- Use fractionated or virgin cold pressed for maximum skin benefit

Interesting fact: In 2008 Virgin Atlantic Airways flew a Boeing 747 in a bio-fuel trial, powering one of its engines on a mixture of coconut and babassu oil!

shea butter

lanolin flakes

lanolin paste

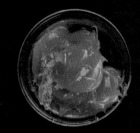

cocoa butter

virgin coconut

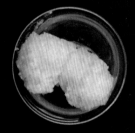

mafura butter

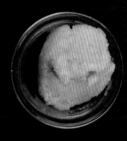

palm butter

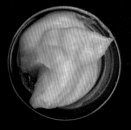

canarium nut butter

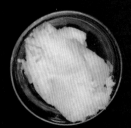

Olive oil

INCI name: Olea europaea

SUGGESTED USE:
Core oil – use at 10–100% of the formula.

Olive oil comes from the fruit and pips of the olive tree. Pure Castile soap is made entirely from olive oil, and Marseilles soap at 72% with other oils and sea water.

Olive oil is classified according to the stages of the pressing. The first pressing, extra virgin, is the purest and clearest. The next pressing is virgin. Both are done without heat or solvents. Then there's pomace grade A, which includes pips, and lastly pomace grade B, which uses a solvent like hexane to extract the last of the oil from the fruit and pips. Each grade of olive oil behaves differently when making soap, and results in a different colour. A super white bar needs to be made from extra virgin or virgin grade oil – the clearest gold in colour. Pomace will give you anything from a creamy off-white colour to a pale olive green. The unsaponifiables in the pomace promote a better reaction with the lye to speed up saponification.

Pomace olive oil can react violently with some essential oils, especially the spice ones, or with fragrances that contain dipropylene glycol in their formula, causing the soap to seize or begin to harden prematurely, so be prepared to rush the soap into the moulds before it is too late.

Olive oil has everything the soap maker needs.

SOAP-MAKING QUALITIES
- Produces a very creamy, mild soap – safe for babies
- Contributes to the hardness of the bar
- Easy to source
- Relatively inexpensive if you use pomace grade
- Provides a stable lather
- The higher the percentage of olive oil, the poorer the lather
- Considered a medium to heavy oil
- Has a good shelf life – over 12 months (more for extra virgin)
- Can be temperamental and unpredictable in soap making
- Best used in conjunction with coconut and palm oils and at 30–40% of the formula
- Takes long to cure
- If using pomace grade, add preservation

EFFECTS ON SKIN

- Helps the skin retain moisture
- Does not block normal pore functions, allowing the skin to sweat and breathe as normal
- Very mild and gentle soap – ideal for babies and highly sensitive skin
- The high level of unsaponifiables is what makes pomace olive oil so good for the skin, as these include the tocopherols (preservatives) and squalene naturally found in our sebum
- Not suitable for acne

Canola/rapeseed oil

INCI name: Brassica napus

SUGGESTED USE:
Core oil – use at 10–25% of the formula.

Canola or rapeseed oil comes from the cabbage-smelling plants that produce beautiful fields of yellow flowers in the Southern hemisphere during August.

SOAP-MAKING QUALITIES

- Slows down trace time – good for special pouring techniques
- Low but creamy lather
- Almost entirely unsaturated (only 6% saturated fats), so needs to be combined with saturated oils to get it to trace
- Very easy to source
- Inexpensive oil – can be added into formula to reduce costs
- Medium shelf life – 12 months

EFFECTS ON SKIN

- Good skin penetration
- Moisturising

Palm oil

INCI name: Elaeis guineensis

SUGGESTED USE:
Core oil – use at 20–40% of the formula.

Palm oil comes from the fruit pulp of a different kind of palm to the coconut palm. Palm oil is a core soap-making oil. It grows in Malaysia but is a controversial oil – growth in Malaysian palm oil production has decimated the habitats of many endangered species, the most emotive one being the orangutan. It is important to fully research your source of palm oil and buy only from very old plantations (see page 16). It is available in various forms:

- **Organic** – no fertilisers or pesticides are used in the growing of the palms.
- **Refined** – processed to deodorise and bleach.
- **Unrefined** – crude, unprocessed.
- **Partially hydrogenated** – pumped with hydrogen to get it to stay solid at room temperature. This is not a natural or advisable option.

SOAP-MAKING QUALITIES
- Use in combination with other oils to prevent a crumbly soap
- Inexpensive and relatively easy to source
- Good shelf life – 12 months and more
- Hardens the bar
- Gives body to the soap
- Produces a low to medium lather, but is slow to lather
- Traces quickly
- Vegetarian substitute for animal tallow

EFFECTS ON SKIN
- Mild cleanser
- Rich in antioxidants, vitamins A and E
- Protects skin cells

Sunflower oil

INCI name: Helianthus annuus

SUGGESTED USE:
Core oil – use at 10–25% of the formula.

This oil is pressed from the seeds of sunflowers. It has a poor shelf life of 3–6 months and needs preservation.

SOAP-MAKING QUALITIES
- Very inexpensive oil – one of the cheapest
- Slow to saponify
- Longer curing and hardening times
- Blends very well with other oils
- Rich, creamy lather
- Very light oil

EFFECTS ON SKIN
- Nicely moisturising
- Contains natural vitamin E tocopherols
- Natural antioxidants
- Vitamins A, D and E
- Forms a protective germ-resistant barrier on the skin
- Helps skin retain water
- Good for acne and can be used on the face

Interesting fact: Studies done on premature babies who were susceptible to infection as a result of their underdeveloped skin, showed that if they were smeared daily with sunflower oil, they were 41% less likely to develop infections.

Avocado oil

INCI name: Persea gratissima

SUGGESTED USE:
Core oil – use at 10–20% of the formula.

Pressed from the fruit of the avocado tree, it is a superb oil with intense moisturising properties. Cold pressed and unrefined is best. It is one of my favourite oils, and in RAIN stores we sell it as a crude oil in our scrub deli bar – you can use it to make body scrubs. It does not, however, add to the hardness of the bar, and the lather is unimpressive.

SOAP-MAKING QUALITIES
- High in unsaponifiables, so it produces a really creamy, rich soap bar that leaves your skin feeling as though you washed with a body lotion
- Traces quickly
- Long shelf life – 12 months plus
- High in tocopherols, which helps retard rancidity
- Medium to heavy oil

EFFECTS ON SKIN
- Vitamins A, B and E
- Highly moisturising and conditioning
- Helps heal dry and damaged skin
- Regenerates skin cells
- Excellent for eczema and extremely sensitive skin
- Easily absorbed into the skin
- Ideal for hair and scalp care as it is easily absorbed by hair strands
- Soothes sunburnt skin

Kalahari melon oil

INCI name: Citrullus lanatus

SUGGESTED USE:

Supplementary or **superfatting oil** – add at trace, 1 heaped tablespoon (15-20 ml) per 2.2 lbs (1 kg) of oils, or 5–10% of the formula (see Superfatting, page 18).

This is one of our favourite oils at RAIN. These wild melons grow in the Kalahari. Filled with life-giving moisture and packed with antioxidants and nutrients, the plant can sustain itself in the extremely harsh desert environment. Indigenous people typically chew the seeds (to release the oils) and rub their skins with a combination of the seed oil and their saliva as a sun-protecting moisturiser. A person can live for six consecutive weeks off the water, seeds and fruit of these melons, and the San would not dream of crossing the desert when the melons are not in fruit.

The melons are harvested by a Fair Trade cooperative of around 3,000 women, who depend on the income from these precious seeds for their livelihood. The oil is expensive and not easy to source, and soap made with this oil has a poor lathering ability.

SOAP-MAKING QUALITIES

- Medium shelf life – about 9–12 months
- Slight hardening of the bar
- Wild harvested, so it's organic
- Not cultivated
- Fair Trade

EFFECTS ON SKIN

- Helps the skin retain moisture
- Regenerates the epidermis
- Very high in antioxidants
- Contributes to the integrity of the cell wall
- Enables suppleness and elasticity
- Cell restructuring properties
- Skin conditioner

tip: Cold process soap is highly alkaline while being made. That, and the different colours of the oils in your recipe, will cause colours to change. Some lighten, some darken, and some change completely. It is wise to experiment first and know what your blend of oils does to a particular colour.

Marula oil

INCI name: Sclerocarya birrea

SUGGESTED USE:
Supplementary or **superfatting oil** – use at 10–15% of the formula, or add at trace at 1% of the formula (see Superfatting, page 18).

The marula tree grows wild in southern Africa and is famous for the creamy liqueur, Amarula, which is made from its fruit. Elephants tend to favour the overripe fruit and become mildly intoxicated from eating it. It is traditionally used by the Tsonga people to moisturise their bodies and massage their babies.

The oil-rich seeds are pressed without solvents to yield light golden oil that is extremely rich in antioxidants. Although expensive, it is one of the Fair Trade wild harvested oils favoured by the RAIN team.

SOAP-MAKING QUALITIES
- High oleic content gives it a long shelf life – about 18–24 months
- Light oil
- Mostly wild harvested
- Fairly easy to source
- Stable
- Nutty aroma

EFFECTS ON SKIN
- Highly nourishing
- High in antioxidants – catechins, tocopherols and flavinoids
- Revitalises skin
- Procyanidin content makes it excellent for hair
- Procyanidins also work at scavenging free radicals before they cause damage to cells
- Moisturising and conditioning

Shea butter

INCI name: Butyrospermum parkii

SUGGESTED USE:
Core butter – use at 5–30% of the formula.

Shea butter comes from the seeds of the karite tree found in West Africa. It is expensive and can be tricky to source.

SOAP-MAKING QUALITIES
- Extremely high in unsaponifiables (11%), making it ideal for soap
- Traces quickly
- Stable lather
- Adds some hardness to the bar
- Can feel a bit sticky if high proportions are used – use in conjunction with cocoa butter to offset this
- May be too oily for some skin types
- Good shelf life – 24 months

EFFECTS ON SKIN
- Highly nourishing
- Intensely moisturising
- Use for extremely dry skin and conditions such as psoriasis, eczema and dandruff

shea butter

Soybean oil

INCI name: Glycine soja

SUGGESTED USE:

Supplementary oil – on its own, it's an unremarkable oil, adding little to the pot. Use at 5–10% of the formula to reduce costs, as it is an inexpensive oil. Use it as you would sunflower oil, but add preservation.

Soybeans are commercially grown to make vegetable shortening.

SOAP-MAKING QUALITIES

- Stable, mediocre lather
- Does not trace quickly
- Light to medium oil
- Short shelf life – about 6–9 months
- Relatively inexpensive
- Easy to find
- Gives a mild, creamy soap bar

EFFECTS ON SKIN

- Nourishing
- Vitamin E softens skin
- Softens hair and prevents flyaway hair
- Moisturising, especially for inflamed skin
- Easily absorbed

Macadamia nut oil

INCI name: Macadamia ternifolia

SUGGESTED USE:

Supplementary oil – use at 5–10% of the formula.

Pressed from the fatty rich nuts of the macadamia tree.

SOAP-MAKING QUALITIES

- Low to medium lather
- Good shelf life – 12 months plus
- Light to medium oil with a non-greasy feeling
- Inexpensive
- Relatively easy to source in the Lowveld region of South Africa where macadamia nuts are grown and the oils pressed

EFFECTS ON SKIN

- Nourishing and skin conditioning
- Contains catechin, which is an antioxidant
- Moisturising
- Reduces transepidermal water loss
- Emollient
- Squalene helps for chapped, cracked skin
- Close to the sebum of the skin
- Good for ageing skin
- The palmitoleic content helps with wounds and burns
- Antimicrobial and antibacterial
- Phytosterols help reduce redness, irritation and itching

Jojoba wax

INCI name: Simmondsia chinensis

SUGGESTED USE:
Supplementary or **superfatting oil** – use at maximum 5%–10% of the formula or at 1–2% at trace as a superfatting oil (see page 18).

Jojoba is technically a wax, not an oil. When whaling became outlawed, jojoba wax replaced the oil from the sperm whale in cosmetic applications. It is expensive and not easy to source, and contains substances that don't saponify, so use sparingly.

SOAP-MAKING QUALITIES
- Low to medium stable lather
- Very stable
- Very long shelf life – 24 months

EFFECTS ON SKIN
- Easily absorbed through hair follicles – it just slides into your skin without blocking anything along the way
- It mixes with natural sebum, allowing the skin to breathe
- Nourishing
- Moisturising and softening
- Anti-inflammatory
- Dry emollient
- Good for hair care because of the way in which it glides into hair follicles
- Antioxidant
- Helps with moisture retention, damage repair and flexibility

Castor oil

INCI name: Ricinus communis

SUGGESTED USE:
Supplementary or **superfatting oil** – add at trace, 1 heaped tablespoon (15-20 ml) per 2.2 lbs (1 kg) of oils. This is one of the best oils to boost lathering at 6 tsp (30 ml) per 2.2 lbs (1 kg) of oils (see Superfatting, page 18). If used as a supplementary oil, use at 5–10% of the formula. Using too much will cause the odour to carry through to the end bar and also make it soft.

Castor oil comes from the beans of the palma christi tree. The first pressing is used for medicine (the oil makes a great laxative). Make sure you have the detoxified version and not raw, unprocessed castor oil. It is high in ricinoleic acid (87%), which makes it highly viscose.

SOAP-MAKING QUALITIES
- Excellent lathering ability
- Helps bind fragrance
- Excellent for hair care and men's shaving products
- Traces fairly quickly
- Fairly inexpensive
- Easy to source
- Very thick oil
- Good shelf life – 12 months plus

EFFECTS ON SKIN
- Provides slip in shaving soap due to its emollient viscosity
- It is a shiny greasy oil used in lipstick and lip gloss
- Penetrates skin easily due to low molecular weight
- Highly moisturising as it is a humectant, drawing moisture to the skin
- Antifungal and antibacterial

Lanolin

INCI name: Lanolin

SUGGESTED USE:
Supplementary or **superfatting** – use 6 tsp
(30 ml) per 2.2 lbs (1 kg) of oils if superfatting, or
2–5% of the formula if used as supplementary.
Add to the melting oils and NOT at trace.

Lanolin is a fat that comes from the wool of
sheep. It is high in allergens, often causing
reactions in sensitive skins. It does not lather,
and contains substances that do not saponify,
so use sparingly.

SOAP-MAKING QUALITIES
- Traces quickly
- Contributes hardness to the bar
- Good shelf life – about 12–18 months

EFFECTS ON SKIN
- Highly nourishing
- Highly emollient
- Repairs cracked, broken skin
- Intensely moisturising

lanolin flakes

Apricot kernel oil

INCI name: Prunus armeniaca

SUGGESTED USE:
Core oil – use at 10–15% of the formula.

SOAP-MAKING QUALITIES
- Low to medium lather
- Good shelf life – 12 months
- Very light
- Interchangeable with sweet almond oil
- No scent
- Brings oleic acid into the mix without olive
  oil's heaviness

EFFECTS ON SKIN
- Nourishes, softens and regenerates cells
- Absorbs easily due to its lightness
- Offers barrier repair support
- Moisturising
- Anti-inflammatory
- Reduces redness and itchiness
- High in vitamin E

tip: Weight and volume are not
the same. We always work with
weight, not volume, when making
soap. For example, a liter (a quart)
of oil weighs roughly 1.8-2 lbs
(830-910 g), not 2.2 lbs (1 kg). Also
bear this in mind when doing your
costing. Weigh the oil you need
for your recipe and pour it into a
measuring jug to see its volume.
To obtain an accurate cost, take
the liter price, divide by 1000 and
multiply by the millilitres you need
for your recipe.

Cocoa butter

INCI name: Theobroma cacao

SUGGESTED USE:
Supplementary or **superfatting** – add at trace, 1 heaped tablespoon (15-20 ml) per 2.2 lbs (1 kg) of oils (see Superfatting, page 18), or at 5–15% of the formula if used as a supplementary butter.

Pressed from the beans of the cocoa tree, which delivers cocoa and chocolate all at the same time!

You can get it in brown or creamy white, like white chocolate, and in a deodorised or non-deodorised form. In the deodorised form, you can still smell chocolate, only less so. Best used with unsaturated oils like avocado and olive. It is fairly expensive and some people can have an allergic reaction to it.

SOAP-MAKING QUALITIES
- Traces quickly
- Helps harden the bar, but it will become too hard and crack if used at over 10% of the formula
- Medium lather
- The fat is very hard and highly saturated
- Strong smell of chocolate, but does not carry through to the soap
- Very good shelf life – about 24–36 months

EFFECTS ON SKIN
- Highly nourishing and enriching
- Easily absorbed
- Intensely moisturising and conditioning

Grapeseed oil

INCI name: Vitis vinifera

SUGGESTED USE:
Core oil – use at 10–20% of the formula.

Pressed from the pips in grapes. It has a short shelf life of 3–6 months, so needs preserving.

SOAP-MAKING QUALITIES
- Low to medium lather
- Inexpensive
- Light, dry oil
- Easy to find in grape-growing regions

EFFECTS ON SKIN
- Helps with barrier repair
- Moisturising
- Anti-inflammatory
- Produces a mild soap

Sweet almond oil

INCI name: Prunus amygdalus dulcis

SUGGESTED USE:
Core oil – use at 10–20% of the formula.

Pressed from the nuts of the almond tree.

SOAP-MAKING QUALITIES
- Low to medium lather
- Medium shelf life – 12 months
- Very light oil
- Interchangeable with apricot kernel oil
- Odourless

EFFECTS ON SKIN
- Nourishing
- Absorbs easily
- Moisturising, softening
- Helps with dry, itching, flaky skin

VOLUME TO WEIGHT RATIOS OF SOME COMMON OILS

Pomace olive oil: 1 quart (1 liter) = 1.92 lbs (870 g)
Extra virgin olive oil: 1 quart (1 liter) = 1.95 lbs (883 g)
Sunflower oil: 1 quart (1 liter) = 1.95 lbs (883 g)
Rosehip oil: 1 quart (1 liter) = 1.96 lbs (890 g)
Jojoba oil: 1 quart (1 liter) = 1.84 lbs (833 g)
Sweet almond oil: 1 quart (1 liter) = 1.92 lbs (873 g)
Grapeseed oil: 1 quart (1 liter) = 1.93 lbs (875 g)
Avocado oil: 1 quart (1 liter) = 1.93 lbs (874 g)
Macadamia nut oil: 1 quart (1 liter) = 2 lbs (910 g)

tip: Pomace olive oil is high in unsaponifiables, and as such, it produces a darker soap than one made with virgin or extra virgin olive oil. Use the higher grades of olive oil for a white soap.

COLOURS OF OILS

Oils lend colour to soap, so choose oils that either deliver a colour of their own or do not detract from the colour effects that you wish to create.

Rosehip oil – peachy pink tones
Unrefined avocado oil – olive green tones
Coconut oil – white
Virgin and extra virgin olive oil – white
Pomace olive oil – off-white
Wheat germ oil – yellowy orange
Unrefined palm oil – yellowy orange
Red palm oil – red
Hemp seed oil – sludgy green

tip: For the whitest soap base possible – use a 75% virgin olive oil and 25% coconut oil mix.

For more comprehensive information on oils and fats, tables on their hard/soft categorisations and their chemical profile, visit the RAIN website (www.rainafrica.com/tutorials).

lye

Lye is an intense alkali that converts the acid of the oils into soap via the process of saponification. We use man-made sodium hydroxide (NaOH), which comes in the form of pearls or flakes and produces a gentle soap once it has cured. Lye is also referred to in this book as caustic soda. It is made from the electrolysis of seawater brine.

It can be tricky to buy this. Some drain cleaners at the hardware shop will be 100% sodium hydroxide – buy only the powdered form with no additives. Soap-making shops sell it, and you can ask your pharmacy or farmers' co-operative to order it for you. Since it is used in the manufacture of the drug 'tik' (methamphetamine), you may be required to prove what you're using it for. It is highly corrosive in its raw form due to its extremely alkaline nature at a pH of 14.

Lye is the catalyst used to convert fats and oils into a new molecular shape via a saponification process resulting in a salt (soap) and natural glycerine. This is how natural glycerine is formed – it is a by-product of soap making. The large palm oil factories in Malaysia make soap for the sole purpose of manufacturing glycerine – this is where their money lies, as glycerine is used in the dynamite industry. They then sell the soap noodles to large soap manufacturers around the world. This worthless by-product then becomes the supermarket soaps we all know – with just a little colour, a little fragrance, a shape and pretty label. This explains why the price of supermarket soap can never compete with handmade artisan soap that retains all its goodness.

Interesting fact: Lye is a dangerous corrosive alkali before soap making, but after saponification it becomes a neutral product (soap), and it no longer exists as lye. By law, it is not even required to be noted on the ingredients label, as it is no longer there!

SAFETY PRECAUTIONS
WHEN WORKING WITH LYE

Lye is not difficult to use, and you shouldn't be afraid of it, but it does require special precautions when storing and handling. It won't kill you unless you drink a fair amount of it, but it will burn your internal organs and place you in critical care. It can severely irritate your eyes, throat and skin if you don't treat it with respect.

Most crafters work with lye in their kitchens. Take care as lye is corrosive and will damage your counter tops and appliances. Kitchens are also places frequented by children, pets and the elderly. Make sure your lye is clearly labelled and out of reach of children. Store dry lye in an airtight plastic container under lock and key.

When working with lye, use rubber or surgical gloves and goggles. If it gets onto your skin, rinse with diluted vinegar water to neutralise its effects. The really nasty part is getting lye splashed into your eyes. It stings like there is no tomorrow and, unless properly rinsed out, can cause permanent damage. Rinse your eyes **immediately** and repeatedly with copious amounts of water.

When lye is combined with a liquid, it turns milky and then begins to emit fumes and generate internal heat. It almost instantly reaches boiling point. So work in a very well ventilated area and avoid inhaling the fumes. I mix the lye and water in a bucket outside, and bring it back inside once it has cooled a little and is ready to use.

tip: Although both are used for soap making, potassium hydroxide (KOH) and sodium hydroxide (NaOH) cannot be used interchangeably. The former is for liquid soaps only.

Always add the lye to the water and not the other way around.

liquid

The liquid is only there to dissolve the lye and to enable it to spread uniformly throughout the oils. Once the lye and liquid have been combined, it is then referred to as the lye solution. The most commonly used liquid is water. If you have access to quality soft natural spring water, use that.

Tap water – may be hard and high in iron particles, which will turn brown at high pH levels.

Distilled water – distilled water is good, or use rain water strained through muslin.

Sea water – used in traditional Marseilles soaps from France. Collect sea water from a clean, unpopulated beach. There are living organisms in sea water, so it should be used as soon as possible and not be stored.

Borehole, well or lake water – these can be used as a memento of a journey.

Floral waters – orange flower and rose are wonderful options. These can be found in Indian bazaars or food speciality shops (they are used for making Turkish delight). Essential oil hydrosols from the distillation process can also be used.

Tea or plant infusions – herbs and plant material can be infused in hot water (like brewing tea) to impart herbal benefits and properties, as well as colour. These are never used hot and must be strained before adding the lye. They may colour your end soap.

Spice water – used for colouring, this will smell really bad when first mixed, but the smell doesn't follow through to the end product.

Beer and coffee – these are also an option, but are not within the scope of this book.

Milk – you can use buttermilk, goat, cow, sheep or donkey milk, camel or buffalo milk, as well as coconut milk. But milks are handled in a very different way – the subject of another book.

tip: All liquids should be well strained and should be cold when adding the lye. Lye generates excessive heat, and adding it to hot water can cause a severe and dangerous eruption.

colourants

The issue of colour is a thorny one. As an artist and creator, you want to achieve special effects with your soap designs, but using natural colourants has very limiting possibilities. Naturals tend to be plentiful in the browny orangey department, very thin on pinks, lilacs and blues, and almost nonexistent on greens (at least ones that don't smell fishy!). You may have to resort to safe synthetics approved by the FDA, but you should never compromise on skin safety. Skin is like a giant sponge – it absorbs everything we put onto it. Artificial colourants and synthetic chemicals are not healthy for our bodies, so choose wisely.

I have divided colourants loosely into naturals and synthetics (though there are grey areas in-between – some, for example, are naturals overlaid with synthetics). Don't assume that because something is natural, it's safe. Naturals may cause allergic reactions if used in large quantities. Allergies are usually caused by natural things – wheat, nuts, milk, poison ivy, etc.

There are FDA-approved skin-safe synthetic cosmetic colourants. Most of them are the colours you use in make-up every day. Interestingly, iron oxide is completely natural, but is forbidden by the FDA as a colourant for skin products due to its high heavy-metal content (including arsenic). Allergies and skin ailments, especially vaginal thrush, are often caused by synthetic dyes in soaps and toilet papers, so use colour with caution.

At RAIN, 90% of our products have either no colourant at all or are coloured using 100% natural colourants. The other 10% have FDA-approved skin-safe synthetic colourants – this can be seen on the labels in the form of a CI number towards the end of an ingredient listing. If we make a label claim that a product is 100% natural, then it always is – including its natural colourant.

Be aware that your colours should never transfer onto towels or face cloths, and the lather of any soap must always be white. Coloured lather indicates extreme dosages of colour and is unsafe for your skin.

tip: Almost inevitably, the intensely alkaline nature of the soap-making reaction alters colours dramatically. Experiment to be sure of the colours you get when you unmould, and also when the soap has cured for four weeks. Don't rely fully on my final results – remember, a chemical reaction is affected by many variables. For example, my skin-safe FDA-approved synthetic turquoise colour delivers a gentle turquoise in liquid and melt-and-pour soaps, as you would expect, but a magnificent royal purple in cold process soap! Test for yourself to be sure.

Also note that all colourants are affected by pH levels, direct light and heat. With naturals, it is even more so. They may fade in light, morph with heat or change as the pH of the soap drops during the curing process.

Using natural colourants is challenging as many of them are difficult to source, expensive, tricky to convert into a useable form, and they deliver inconsistent and unpredictable results. For the home crafter, I have used both natural colourants and a few safe D&C (drug and cosmetic) colours in this book. Natural colourants can be sourced in your kitchen or garden, in health shops, and ordered online. Luckily they are light and cost little to post from anywhere in the world. Synthetic colourants can largely be sourced at soap-making shops, baking shops and online.

Before claiming an all-natural product, be sure to research the nature of the colourants you are using as what you think is natural may in fact be a synthetic version of the natural with the same name.

St Helens lahar mud

Canadian glacial mud

Great Barrier Reef mud

NATURAL COLOURANTS

Natural colours are weaker than synthetics and you need larger quantities to obtain results. So err on the side of generosity when using naturals. However, exercise caution with spices, as generous doses may cause allergic reactions.

Naturals need to be handled in different ways in order to coax them to release their colours. Some release more readily into the liquid part of the recipe, some into the lye solution, some into the oils, and some as a powder to be added at trace. Please consult the table of naturals to see which methods work best for which material, to be found at www.rainafrica.com/tutorials.

In general, naturals deliver dirty, muddy colours and not crisp, pure, primary colours or neons. I prefer the earthy, natural look to the brights of synthetic colourants, but it is a matter of personal taste.

Herbs, teas and spices often leave tiny speckles of colour in the soap and do not yield a solid colour. This can be extremely pleasing aesthetically, but may not be the look you are after.

When mixing dried material into the soap batter at trace, the powders tend to clump and don't blend. Rather place the powder and a small spoon of batter into a little dish, where you can agitate it sufficiently to get it to blend fully, and then incorporate the small batch of coloured batter into the main batch.

Micas

These are silicate minerals from rock and crystals mined from the earth. Sometimes they are not truly natural as they are sold as a white rock powder which has been coated with unnatural FD&C (food, drug and cosmetic) colours and pigments – the grey area mentioned earlier.

micas

Micas have reflective qualities (a slight shimmer) and so are ideal for translucent soap where they perform like ballet dancers on stage. They are used in most eye shadows, lipsticks, nail varnishes, blushes, mascaras, foundations, and were also used in ancient cave paintings!

· Stable at high temperatures
· Stable in moisture
· Stable in light
· Don't sparkle in CP (cold process) and HP (hot process) soap
· Don't form lumps, so blend easily
· Some are unreliable in producing predictable results, like reds, silver and greens (see below)
· Yellows, blues and purples tend to work well
· If you mix the colour into a little glycerine to suspend it, and then into your lye water before adding the oils, the colour you see is the colour you'll get, preventing expensive mistakes
· Normal dosage: maximum of 1 tsp (5 ml) per 2.2 lbs (1 kg) of soap

tip: Purists will question the natural claim of your micas, so investigate your source thoroughly to know if you are using the natural or synthetic ones.

silver

imperial red

ruben

Ochres and clays

Ochres are naturally tinted clays that contain mineral oxides. They are often used medicinally and in make-up, and were also used for ancient cave paintings. Ochres come in many different tones of reds, yellows and browns. They are considered more a clay than a mineral. I find 1–2 tablespoons is sufficient for a 2.2 lb (1 kg) batch, but you can add more for greater intensity of colour.

Clays are highly absorbent. They work magnificently as natural colourants and are my favourites. Clays such as bentonite, Australian red, Brazilian pink, kaolin, atlas, French green and rhassoul are also used as masks as they can absorb and cleanse. Excessive clay in soap can be drying to the skin. Shaving soaps benefit from the inclusion of bentonite as it produces a slip effect to the lather to help the razor glide.

Clay can be added at light trace at about 2-4 tsp (10-20 ml) per 2.2 lbs (1 kg) of oils. Place the clay in a small bowl, add a little traced soap to the clay and blend it into a paste. Add the lump-free paste to the master batch of traced soap and pour into the moulds.

Clays give subtle colours to natural soap. A myriad of colours are mined all over the world. Make it a hobby to search for cosmetic-grade clays wherever you travel. They are often sold in food markets for festivals as they are used for body decorations. Indian bazaars often carry clay powders for use at Divali and Holi festivals.

40

Resins and gum

Resins and gum are the solidified sap from trees and shrubs. They often have medicinal properties and some, like frankincense, myrrh and omumbiri, have exquisite fragrances. Others are rosin, benzoin, styrax, gum arabic and balsam of Peru. They yield mostly rich brown tones and darken the colours of soap. They come as hard lumps which need to be powdered. The powder will not blend with water, oil or lye solution as it is. It has to be suspended in as little alcohol as possible (alcohol tends to seize the soap batter) and be added very swiftly at trace. You have to be quick if you want to get batter with resins into the moulds before the mixture seizes.

The strong-smelling resins (oleoresins) impart their own fragrances to the soap, so bear this in mind when choosing fragrances. They are usually expensive and tricky to work with and sometimes produce a grainy bar.

gum   resin

Oxides

Oxides are pretty stable and cheap. They tend to clump though, so blend into an oil or glycerine base, strain through muslin and bottle for later use.

Iron oxide can be mined, but can also come from rust. Although technically natural, the FDA does not approve iron oxides for use on skin due to their heavy metal and arsenic content. But there are safe oxides like titanium dioxide found in most cosmetics and sunscreens. This is a lovely white pigment that is used to create opaque soap and to colour natural soap batter (which is almost always a creamy colour) to a white base to show true colour results when adding other colourants. It is an indispensable item in your colour toolbox. Pre-blend oxides into oil for use in CP and HP soap (see Ultramarines, page 49).

Natural chrome oxide green, made from a mineral called eskolaite, is a safe oxide and essential for the green palette. It is rare and expensive, so most commercially available chromium oxides are man-made synthetics. It produces a deep, stable, predictable green colour. Purists should hunt down the natural version from Finland.

Zinc oxide – a white pigment – has antibacterial and antifungal properties and provides a natural sunscreen.

tip: Purists will question you on the naturalness of your oxides, so be sure to know the source.

titanium dioxide

pumice   charcoal

Pumice and charcoals

Pumice is volcanic rock. Ground to a fine powder, it will produce a slightly grainy exfoliating soap of various shades of browny grey.

Charcoal is made by burning wood or bamboo at extremely high temperatures 1832°F (1000°C). This is then ground into a fine powder or dust and provides tones of grey to black. It has a grainy, exfoliating effect on the soap bar, but has the added benefit of being a detoxifying agent. It is the only way to achieve a natural grey or blue-grey colour.

Use ground pumice and charcoals at 1-3 tsp (5-15 ml) per 2.2 lbs (1 kg) of soap. If you want a heavily exfoliating soap for a gardener or artist, be generous with the medium.

Herbs, flowers, roots and seeds

These can be fresh, or dry and powdered. Herbs usually leave tiny speckles in soap and don't produce an evenly blended colour. Most herbs tend to go brown with time, so it's best to have them as fine as possible to avoid an ugly bar.

Fresh herbs are usually used to infuse in the liquid phase of the recipe. Use large quantities to get the herbal benefits of the plants infused into the water or oil. With water infusions, make a very strong tea brew and allow to cool and steep before straining. With oil infusions, heat the oil and use 9 parts oil to 1 part plant material. Allow to steep for a week before straining and using. Make sure the herbs have not been sprayed with pesticides, and that they are washed and bug free.

butterfly pea

Powdered herbs should be ground as finely as possible to reduce the speckling effect on the soap, then stirred into a mini sample of the batter to disperse the powder, and then added to the master batch – just as you would do with all other powders. A coffee grinder or pestle and mortar are usually readily available, but will not produce the finest powder necessary to avoid speckling. Have the material commercially ground by a spice house to achieve best results. What you can do, however, is pass the powdered material through a fine tea strainer to remove the bigger bits. You ideally want the powdered dust.

Use the herbs you would use in cooking, plus plants from which essentials are extracted – these have medicinal and health benefits.

Cocoa powder works well as a soap colourant and should be pre-blended in a small amount of soap batter before being added.

Coffee tends to impart a coffee smell and a grainy texture to the soap, and if this is not what you are after, avoid it. Coffee is an odour absorber, so a soap coloured with coffee grounds can be marketed as an odour-absorbent soap. Use filtered grain-free coffee water in place of the normal lye water to reinforce the colour.

Annatto seeds need to be infused in warm oil for a few hours and then strained out. They give a vague orangey colour, but I have not found them effective at all.

cocoa

43

Spices

Spices are really super when combined and used in a chai soap. They produce mainly yellows to oranges, browns and peachy tones.

Turmeric works really well as a natural colourant, and can be infused into the oils or added directly to the batter in a paste. It has a slight odour, but you can mask it with fragrance.

Paprika (sweet pepper) produces a lovely rusted peachy colour. Infuse it into the oil at 2 tsp (10 ml) per 2.2 lbs (1 kg) of oils. It leaves a mild earthy odour.

Nutmeg delivers a soft beige colour with no offensive odour, and cinnamon a darker version.

Cloves give a similar earthy tone, but the odour tends to carry through.

turmeric

paprika

nutmeg

cloves

mangosteen

lemon peel

Fruit and vegetable powders

Dried powdered fruits and vegetables like mangosteen, wheat grass powder, olive leaf powder, beta carotene and beetroot have mixed results. Some of these can be bought from specialist health shops.

Beta carotene comes from carrots and egg yolks and is high in antioxidants. It is extremely expensive – use at .20 tsp (1 ml) per 2.2 lb (1 kg) batch, dissolved in a little water before adding. It produces an orange colour.

Don't expect beetroot to deliver burgundy in either its powdered or liquid form. I have tried drying the stalks, leaves and root and grinding them to powders, I have tried infusions – you simply do not get the colour. But you do get a pretty ivory colour!

Mangosteen powder can be used at 4 tsp (20 ml) per 2.2 lb (1 kg). I use this colourant very successfully, but it's not easy to find.

Olive leaf powder (dried and ground leaves of the olive tree) can be added directly to the batter at 2 tsp (10 ml) per 2.2 lb (1 kg) batch.

Orange or lemon rind powder works quite well as the soap takes on an orangey colour and the rind adds a bit of exfoliating texture and a vague citrus scent to the soap. Use at least 1-2 tsp (5-10 ml) per 2.2 lbs (1 kg) of soap.

You will have to dehydrate all vegetable matter properly in a low oven or in the sun before attempting to grind it. Even slightly moist material will not grind. Grind as finely as possible and strain to remove bigger pieces. Laboratories that manufacture vitamins and medicines are a good place to source these natural powders.

Seaweed and plant algae

I do not like the odours left by algae and seaweeds. Make your own call on this one. Natural green is difficult to achieve, so you're sometimes forced to use these options.

The seaweed sheets you find in supermarkets or Chinese food shops (used to make sushi) are ideal. These are normally nori (Porphyra). They are high in minerals and vitamins and can be used finely powdered. They tend to have the same effect as herbs – leaving a speckled finish to the soap. Use 2 tsp (10 ml) for a 2.2 lb (1 kg) batch.

Spirulina (Arthrospira platensis) is a seaweed found in powdered form in health shops, while Athrospira maxima is a tropical lake alga rich in vitamins and minerals. Both add strong colour – the former a deep, sludgy green and the latter a lovely bluey green, but they can leave a definite musty, fishy undertone that you will need to mask with a healthy percentage of a herbal green fragrance and see if the end result pleases you. Use 2 tsp (10 ml) powder per 2.2 lb (1 kg) soap batch.

Kelp (Phaeophyceae) is high in nutrients and can be used to achieve a soft tone of pale sage, but also has the fishy odour.

Chinese medicine shops use many other species of seaweed and freshwater algae, whole or powdered, for their medicinal properties. Experiment with them individually or in combination.

algae

green algae

seaweed

nori seaweed

cruelty alert: The female cochineal, a scale insect, is bred and farmed in Peru and Mexico where it thrives on prickly pear plantations. It is crushed and used to make a bright carmine pink colourant for food and cosmetics. Public resistance to artificial colourants has seen the resurgence of the cochineal farming industry to offer a natural colourant. Even Starbucks use it in their strawberry drinks. Think twice before you eat or drink pink! We at RAIN are fanatical about the killing of animals and never use this natural colourant.

Teas

Rooibos and honeybush teas make wonderful additives as they are high in antioxidants. Ground teas don't actually dissolve and don't really impart their full colour to the soap batter, but rather tend to speckle the soap – unless you can lay your hands on tea dust, which is extremely finely ground.

Asian markets are filled with all sorts of medicinal and green teas. Most large cities have a mini Chinatown. Visit them to source interesting varieties of plant materials.

Safflower is a tea found in Asia, or in Chinese supermarkets. We use this a lot for colouring. The powdered form is a great natural colourant – add 2 tsp (10 ml) per 2.2 lb (1 kg) batch directly to the batter.

Hibiscus tea (roselle) can be infused in water and left for a week or two to steep. The beetroot-coloured water gives soap an interesting caramel-fudge colour that looks truly edible. The hibiscus also has excellent skin properties (see Rescue, page 84).

Anchan or violet tea makes striking purple water that adds a greyish tone to soap.

MAKING HERBAL INFUSIONS

This method of extraction is used for herbs, flowers, leaves, seeds and teas. Herbs can be infused in oil, alcohol or other liquids such as milk. For soap-making purposes, we don't use alcohol as that tends to seize the soap. You infuse herbs to gain something from them, for example a colour, a special medicinal property or an active ingredient.

To make infusions, you will need:
- Dried plant material
- A chosen oil or other liquid (water, milk)
- Means of heating – hot plate, kettle or microwave
- Wooden spoon or spatula
- Funnel with muslin or cheesecloth to strain
- A sterilised glass bottle for storing the infusion

WATER OR MILK INFUSIONS

The ratio is 9 parts boiling liquid to 1 part dried material. For fresh material, you use 7 parts boiling liquid to 3 parts fresh material. Think of it as making a very strong pot of tea. Allow to steep for a few hours till cool. Strain and use as the liquid part of your soap recipe.

OIL INFUSIONS

The ratio is 9 parts hot oil to 1 part dried material. For fresh material, you use 7 parts hot oil to 3 parts fresh material. The oil should be more than warm but not overly hot as it could scald the delicate material. Allow to steep for a few hours, or a week and longer for dried material. Strain and use as the oil part of your soap recipe.

SYNTHETIC COLOURANTS

In general, synthetic colours stain clothes, hands and even work surfaces. Be careful when you work with them. Protect your clothes and counter tops. Always add these colours one drop at a time. They are intense. You can always add colour, but you can't take it out. As a guideline, use .4-1 tsp (2-5 ml) per 2.2 lb (1 kg) batch.

D&C colourants

If you're making soaps commercially, you are accountable for the safety of your customers. So, when using D&C colourants, request an MSDS (material safety data sheet) from the supplier. Read it and keep it on file. At the same time, request the registered CI (colour index) number for that colour, as this information will, by law, need to appear on the ingredient listing on the label of the soap. CI numbers are universally recognised numbers for commercial products using colours. A CI number does not necessarily imply that the colour is skin safe – that can only be ascertained from the MSDS.

D&C colours are highly concentrated and just .2 tsp (1 ml) of colour is enough to colour a 6.6 lb (3 kg) batch of soap. They are quite stable and predictable and the colours last. There is a large variety to choose from and they are really easy to work with.

I premix large batches into either an oil or a water base, depending on whether I'll be using it in CP, HP or M&P. I place the bulk dilution into a sterilised glass container and label it. Then I formulate my recipes from the bulk dilution so as to maintain colour consistency over long periods of time.

FD&C colourants

Food colours come in powder, liquid or gel form. They can be bought at baking shops and in supermarkets. Although I don't advise it, you can use food colours in soap making . But they are not designed for the intense lye solution and often produce disappointing results. They fade quickly and also tend to stain baths and basins. They also bleed between layers. I really wouldn't recommend food colours if you're planning to sell your soaps. They would only be suitable for own use or personal gifts.

Lab colours

These are found on overseas mail order sites and are FD&C colours which have been pre-blended into a liquid form for convenience. If you want to buy them, choose the varieties that have been formulated for a high pH soap process – these are hardier and more stable for CP and HP soaps.

Glitter

Glitter's highly synthetic nature puts me off, and I don't advise using it. Made from polyester, it will melt if heated. It's best used in translucent soap to show off its sparkle. In CP, add it only at the coolest point of trace, in little sprinkles like salt on an egg.

Synthetic pigments

These produce rather intense colours, using roughly 1-2 tsp (5-10 ml) of colour per 6.6 lb (3 kg) batch. They can be blended together to make your own colours and shades.

Ultramarines (pinks, blues and violets) used to be completely natural and were obtained from powdered lapis lazuli, but are now synthetically manufactured. They are non-toxic synthetics, and are safe to use on skin. You need just 1 tsp (5 ml) of ultramarine to colour a 6.6 lb (3 kg) batch of soap. Ultramarines are not affected by lye, so can be blended into lye water without complications.

Red, brown, black oxides are all variant colours of iron oxides and can be found in nature, but are high in heavy metals such as arsenic and mercury and should not be used. Synthetic versions are available. Oxides tend to clump, and don't blend with water and alcohol, so need to be pre-blended into an oil or glycerine base before being incorporated into the soap batter. Choose one of the options below, bottle in a sterilised glass jar, label and use as required. Shelf life is 6–9 months. Use these blends at 2 tsp (10 ml) colour per 2.2 lbs (1 kg) for CP and HP soap.

OIL OPTION (FOR USE IN CP AND HP ONLY):
- 5.4 TB (80 ml) (choose one with a long shelf life, like jojoba, olive, avocado or sweet almond)
- 1 tsp (5 ml) colour

GLYCERINE OPTION (FOR USE IN CP, HP AND M&P):
- 5.4 TB (80 ml) liquid glycerine
- ½ tsp (2.5 ml)

For both options, mix thoroughly but gently to avoid the colour powder clumping. Blend well with a whisk or a small battery-operated cappuccino frother.

tip: Never ever use candle colourants, artist pigments, clay glaze colours or clothing dyes. Most of these are not safe for skin.

fragrance

Fragrance is the soul of soap, elevating it from being a functional item to something that offers aesthetic engagement. It stimulates our sense of smell, and with that comes a myriad of emotional responses and memories or connections. It is meaningful to people and purchasing choices are frequently made on fragrance alone.

Fragrance is divided into two categories – naturals (essential oils) and naturally derived synthetics (perfumes).

Essential oils are highly concentrated, powerful, volatile chemical compounds extracted by various means from all parts of specific plants, including roots, leaves, flowers, fruits, sap and seeds. Sometimes these oils appear to form part of the plant's immune system. They are natural and offer medicinal and healing properties.

Perfumes are man-made, using essential oils, distillates of essential oils, naturally derived resins and plant compounds, but with added fixatives and solvents. Many synthetic elements in perfumes have been man-made for various and very valid reasons:

- To negate the highly controversial and emotive issues around the use of compounds from animals. I would never endorse the use of genuine musk, civet or ambergris – give me the synthetic versions any day!
- To provide a fragrance note where the genuine thing is prohibitively expensive – rose absolute, for instance, costs tens of thousands of US dollars per kilogram.
- To protect sensitive natural resources – where a rare plant could be wiped out if no synthetic version was available.
- To provide a fragrance without the accompanying allergens of the natural version.

While perfumes are fragrant, more user-friendly, often less expensive, easier to source and more versatile, they cannot offer the medicinal and aromatherapeutic qualities of essential oils. At RAIN we use both as we feel each has a place in the fragrancing of body products and soaps, depending on the result you want to achieve.

QUANTITIES

Broadly speaking, essential oils are more powerful and can be used at 0.5–2% of the formula. Perfumes can be used at 1.5–4% of the formula. So in a 2.2 lb (1 kg) batch, at 1% dilution, you would use roughly 2 tsp (10 ml) (this doesn't take into account the weights of different oils, but is a simple enough guideline from which to work.)

Both perfumes and essential oils are added just after trace – this is the point when saponification has taken place and the intensity of the caustic solution is subdued.

POTENTIAL PROBLEMS

Some oils and perfumes may react strongly with the highly alkaline freshly traced soap batter, causing it to thicken rapidly and seize. Always have your moulds and jugs ready so that you can react quickly if you see the mixture seizing and get the batter into the moulds before it's too late. The soap isn't necessarily ruined, just impossible to handle.

Some fragrances fade rapidly, don't make it through the curing process, or may cause discolouration and streaking. You'd need to experiment on small sample batches to see what works and what doesn't.

Fragrances and essential oils are aggressive and can ruin a work surface, so handle with care.

tip: If you're doing fancy pouring techniques, it is a good idea not to add the fragrance to the master batch, but to the separate mini-batches just before pouring them. This will help delay thickening of the batter, which you need in a fancy pour.

tip: Vanilla fragrance or any perfume containing vanillin will turn a white soap brown without any colourant added.

tip: Always add fragrance last as floral fragrances accelerate trace, depriving you of time to play.

PERFUMES

Perfumes are a blend of many ingredients – sometimes between 80 and 150. These ingredients are sourced in nature and are a blend of essential oils, distillates and organics derived from essential oils, as well as synthetic copies of fragrance notes that are prohibitively expensive, have an unsustainable source, or are of animal origin. So synthetics are not all bad news.

I like to think of perfume as a symphony. When you listen to a symphony, you hear various musical instruments producing the sounds. Perfume too, is made from many single notes, like a rose note or a lavender note. The perfumer can be compared to a composer bringing in top, middle and bass notes to create a harmonious sound – a composition.

Perfumes also have top, middle (heart) and base notes. Certain compositions, in order to achieve a particular result (for example a heavily exotic amber/patchouli/musky fragrance), may have a large base note and small top note. Another composition, which aims at freshness and lightness, may have a small base note but large top note. Top notes are what you first smell when you smell a perfume and they tend to evaporate faster than base notes. Base notes start showing through after some time, even hours.

There are different broad categories of perfume (the gourmand or food-fragrance category is a modern trend in perfumery):

Green – crushed green leaves, cucumber
Woody – cedarwood, sandalwood
Citrus – lemon, orange, bergamot
Floral – jasmine, rose, neroli
Aldehydic – tobacco, leather, wood tar, honey
Spicy – cinnamon, ginger
Herbal – rosemary, basil
Ambered/oriental – ambergris, musk
Musky – animalic
Chypre – oak moss, labdanum, patchouli
Fougere – fern-like and herbaceous
Fruity – peach, mango, pear, guava
Gourmand – smelling of food such as vanilla, coffee or chocolate
Aquatic/oceanic – marine scents of lichen, broom

tip: Fragrances with strong base notes last better through the highly alkaline soap-making process.

ESSENTIAL OILS

When extracting essential oils from plants, different methods are used for different plants.

Cold pressing is the best option for producing quality oil, as this causes the least amount of harm to the oils. Oils are pressed through sheer weight from the plant material. This method cannot be used for all plants and also doesn't produce very good yields.

Steam distillation is used for most essential oil extractions. Heat from the steam through a distillation plant breaks down tissue and releases the volatile oils. A by-product of this process is hydrosol, which is the water collected from the steam generated during the distillation process. It is wonderful stuff that is often discarded, so it is normally cheap or free and can be used to replace the water part of the soap formula.

Solvent extraction is a method used for extremely delicate plants that are reluctant to release their precious oils, but oils extracted by means of hexane or other solvents are not classified as natural in the purest sense of the word.

Enfleurage is a method whereby delicate flower petals are placed onto a layer of butter fat and replaced daily for several months. The fragile fragrance is then imparted into the fat, which is then rendered down to an absolute or a concrete. It is a very old-fashioned labour-intensive method still pursued by purists in making all-natural perfumes.

tip:
Floral fragrances
accelerate trace.

It's important to be sure of the quality of the oils you buy. Organic is expensive, but best.

AROMATHERAPY

The inhalation of essential oils has long been used as a kind of rescue remedy (think of smelling salts), and to restore emotional balance, which in turn has a positive effect on stress levels and even physical ailments. This is known as aromatherapy.

My non-medical explanation is that when you smell an essential oil, the olfactory nerves gather the aroma from the tiny molecules, which then travel to the alveoli with their fine blood vessels. There gases are exchanged – oxygen for carbon dioxide – and particles of the essential oils are sent into the blood stream. This stimulates the brain and limbic system where all our emotions and memories are archived, releasing neurotransmitters such as serotonin, hormones and endorphins. There you have it!

tip: Marry your colours and fragrances. Use vanilla in a brown soap and rose in a pink soap and not vice versa.

Some commonly used essential oils

BERGAMOT *Citrus bergamia*

- Perfume note – top
- Extraction – cold pressing
- Price – expensive
- Other – fragrance is fragile and does not hold well; support with Litsea cubeba or lemongrass (see page 59)

Pressed from the fruit of the Citrus bergamia tree, bergamot is used to uplift, relax and refresh. Perfumers use it because it has the properties that allow it to modify and harmonise complex scent combinations. It has a clean, citrus fragrance with a softly spicy undertone. It carries fairly well in soap.

CAPE CHAMOMILE *Eriocephalus punctulatus*

- Perfume note – middle
- Extraction – steam distillation
- Price – extremely expensive
- Other – safe in second trimester of pregnancy and safe for babies

This exquisitely blue oil is from a rare aromatic shrub indigenous to the Cape mountains of South Africa. Valued for its intense fragrance, it is extremely expensive to distil despite successful cultivation as a commercial crop. It alleviates stress, depression and anxiety. The presence of linalyl acetate in the oil means it has similar properties to lavender as a sleep enhancer and relaxant. It also acts as an anti-inflammatory.

CAPE MALVA/ROSE GERANIUM *Pelargonium graveolens*

- Perfume note – middle
- Extracted – steam distillation
- Price – expensive

This oil has a balancing effect on moods, so can be used as a natural anti-depressant. It originally comes from the Koo valley in the Montagu area of the Cape, but is now grown worldwide, especially in the Middle East. The political uprisings in that region have caused the price to quadruple over a 12-month period. It has a rose fragrance. It holds well in soap.

LAVENDER *Lavendula abrialis*

- Perfume note – middle
- Extraction – steam distillation
- Price – affordable
- Other – safe in second trimester of pregnancy and safe for babies

Lavender is one of the most widely used oils on the market and is a favourite of all generations. It holds well in soap making. It has a sweet, camphor-like smell with slightly balsamic overtones. It has the added benefit of combining well with a range of oils. It offers sedation and relaxation, and can calm heart palpitations. It's super mild for babies.

PEPPERMINT *Mentha piperita*

- Perfume note – top
- Extraction – steam distillation
- Price range – inexpensive
- Other – avoid during breastfeeding; fragrance holds well

Peppermint has a powerful menthol aroma that holds extremely well in soap making. It should be used at low percentages as it can be a skin irritant.

SWEET ORANGE *Citrus aurantium*

- Perfume note – top
- Extraction – cold pressed
- Price – inexpensive
- Other – although you can use large percentages, the fragrance does not hold well – support it with some added Litsea cubeba or lemongrass

Sweet orange oil has a fruity aroma and is often used in perfumes. It can relieve tension and depression and generally brighten the mood. It also acts as a muscle relaxant and an immune system booster. The oil is used as a skin tonic, drawing out toxins and dealing well with dry skin and wrinkles. It can, however, become an irritant if used for prolonged periods in large doses. It holds up well in soap making.

EUCALYPTUS *Eucalyptus smithii*

- Perfume note – top
- Extraction – steam distillation
- Price – inexpensive
- Other – fragrance holds well

This South African species has 80% cineole – the magic ingredient that gives eucalyptus most of its valuable properties. It is used in ointments for various ailments, often combined with ingredients like camphor. It has a very sharp and distinctive aroma and should be used with care – it is not recommended for people with high blood pressure or epilepsy. The oil is said to enhance concentration and aid the nervous system. It also has a calming effect on the emotions, is effective for use on burns and is suitable for children.

GINGER *Zingiber officinale*

- Perfume note – base
- Extraction – steam distillation
- Price – expensive
- Other – safe for pregnancy

Ginger has a warm, spicy aroma. This oil can be used to sharpen the senses and cheer you up. It aids circulation and can relieve symptoms of angina as well as bruising and sores.

CINNAMON *Cinnamomum zeylanicum*

- Perfume note – base
- Extraction – steam distillation
- Price – affordable

Avoid cinnamon bark oil – it can cause unpleasant skin reactions. Cinnamon leaf oil is widely used. It is quite powerful and should be treated with respect. It alleviates feelings of weakness, exhaustion and depression and is said to enhance reasoning ability. It has a pep-me-up effect on the whole body, specifically the circulatory system, and offers excellent resistance to viral infections. It can be effective as a skin toner.

TEA TREE *Melaleuca alternifolia*

- Perfume note – middle
- Extraction – steam distillation
- Price – affordable
- Other – fragrance holds well

Tea tree is known for its properties as an antiseptic and treatment for skin ailments. It is used to treat burns, boils, bites and ear infections, but must not be used in the ears. It refreshes and revitalises the mind.

BLACK PEPPER *Piper nigrum*

- Perfume note – middle
- Extraction – steam distillation
- Price – expensive

This is a low-risk oil – the only major precaution is that sudden use in too great quantities can result in over-stimulated kidneys. There's also a minor possibility of skin irritation. The scent is sharp and spicy. The oil is very good to use before sporting activities as it is a vasodilator and gets rid of muscular aches and pains. It is good for stomach ailments and also restores the 'va-va-voom' of the mind and nerves.

Interesting fact: A study in Japan found that citrus essential oil caused data capturers to make fewer mistakes. Another study in the USA showed that peppermint oil increased the accuracy of taste-testers by 25%.

MANDARIN *Citratus madurensis*

- Perfume note – top
- Extraction – cold pressed
- Price – inexpensive
- Other – fragrance does not hold well; add Litsea cubeba or lemongrass for substance; safe for pregnancy and babies

This oil has a sweet, citrus scent with a little tang. It is slightly phototoxic and so it is best not to use it before going into strong sunlight. It alleviates depression and is good for stomach complaints. When used in combination with neroli and lavender it can be an effective remedy for stretch marks and scarring.

LEMONGRASS *Cymbopogon citrates*

- Perfume note – top
- Extraction – steam distillation
- Price – inexpensive
- Other – fragrance holds well

This oil has a strong aroma of lemon and grass. In high percentages, it can irritate the skin. It's a perfect skin toner and body tonic and acts as an astringent by closing pores.

ROSEMARY *Rosmarinus officinalis*

- Perfume note – middle
- Extraction – steam distillation
- Price – affordable
- Other – fragrance holds well

Rosemary oil has a very strong camphor-like smell. It has a stimulating effect, relieves mental strain and increases alertness. It helps prevent dandruff and tightens sagging skin.

NEROLI BLEND *Citrus aurantium*

Interesting fact: To produce less than half a quart (liter) of essential oil, you need:

51 lbs (23 kg) of eucalyptus
152 lbs (69 kg) of lavender
503 lbs (228 kg) of rosemary
1003 lbs (455 kg) of jasmine
2006 lbs (910 kg) of rose

Perhaps that explains the price differences!

· Perfume note – middle to base
· Extraction – steam distillation
· Price – extremely expensive
· Other – safe for pregnancy and babies

This exquisite floral oil is hugely expensive to produce – a mass of flowers produces a mere cup of precious oil. Used as a sedative to calm the nervous system and to relax the body. It is a deodorant, helps fade scarring and stretch marks and is great for dry, sensitive, wrinkled and mature skin.

JASMINE BLEND *Jasminum grandiflorum*

· Perfume note – middle to base
· Extraction – solvent
· Price – extremely expensive
· Other – safe in second trimester of pregnancy, avoid during breastfeeding

Jasmine is a delicate flower, harvested at night to preserve the intensity of the fragrance. Extraction is tricky and laborious, with low yields, making it extremely expensive. It revitalises skin, increasing elasticity and helping to fade stretch marks and scars.

VANILLA BLEND *Vanilla planifolia*

· Perfume note – base
· Extraction – harvested from a resin extracted from the cured vanilla bean over a six-month period
· Price – inexpensive

Vanilla is very popular oil, with strong sentimental connotations. The fragrance is deep, rich, sweet, somewhat woody and animalic, with balsamic, spicy body notes.

Precautions

Essential oils are not simply fragrances, but are intense active compounds that can be harmful if not used correctly. Inform yourself about the safe use of the oils you've chosen. A comprehensive reference book is required when working with essential oils. The knowledge surrounding essential oils is too vast for the scope of this book.

Some oils may irritate the skin, especially sensitive skin. If irritation occurs, discontinue use. Do a small patch test on your inner forearm to see if it is likely to irritate your skin. Oils that may cause irritation are cedarwood, cinnamon, eucalyptus, ginger, lemongrass and peppermint.

Storage

Essential oils are all natural with no preservatives, so they need special care. They loathe sun and light, which is why they are packed in dark bottles. Keep them cool as far as possible. Keep lids tightly closed. Oils can be stored for 1–2 years. For them to be at their best, use within 6–12 months of opening.

Best essential oils for soap making

Citrus oils do not hold up well in the highly alkaline environment of freshly traced soap. The only two that work are lemongrass and Litsea cubeba. You can support other citrus oils with a small measure of these two, to make the mix more robust, or you can reserve citrus oils for rebatching and hand milling techniques (see page 86) where you are adding them to already cured or lower pH soap.

The heavier aromas with large base notes – like sandalwood, cedarwood, patchouli, palmarosa and vanilla – work well with soap.

other additives

Additives are used for one or more of these reasons:
- As **emollients** for added moisture (see Oils and butters, page 15)
- as **exfoliants** for removing dead skin cells
- to **benefit skin** – antibacterial/wound-healing properties
- to improve **lathering**, to **thicken** or **harden** soap
- as **preservation**
- for **visual effect**

Use additives in moderation – they should be an addition, not the centrepiece of your soap.

Many of the additives can be found in the Nature's Choice range at Dis-Chem.

tip: Add the exfoliants at trace as the thicker mixture helps to suspend them in the batter and they don't all fall to the bottom.

EMOLLIENTS

Lanolin, shea butter, cocoa butter and mafura butter are all rich, buttery substances that can be added to the soap just after trace in what is known as superfatting (see Oils and butters, page 15, for details).

EXFOLIANTS

These have slightly abrasive qualities, feel rough on the skin and help to slough away dead skin cells.

Poppy seeds

Great for a grey speckled effect and a mild exfoliant. Because poppy seeds have no sharp edges, they don't scratch like other seeds do when used as an exfoliant.

Luffa

The dried, spongy cucumber-like fruit of the Luffa aegyptiaca plant can be added whole and will look attractive when you slice your loaf, or you can add tiny ones to each bar. You can finely chop the luffa and sprinkle it into the soap. Luffa is a gentle exfoliant.

Sea sand

Choose clean, fine, white sea sand as a mild exfoliant. Sieve to be sure there's no debris.

Bran

Digestive bran is a nice mild exfoliant. Add at trace.

Berry seeds

Dried pomegranate, strawberry and raspberry seeds can be used as mild exfoliants.

Citrus rind

Dried and finely grated rind of any citrus fruits can be added as a mild astringent exfoliant.

Charcoal dust

Charcoal dust delivers multiple benefits to soap. It is used as an exfoliant, but also works to absorb odours. Use finely powdered dust at 2–5%. It will colour your end soap.

Pumice stone powder

Use as an exfoliant. The colour of the powder will depend on the source of the pumice, which is volcanic rock and can be pink, brown, grey or black.

EFFECTS ON SKIN

Honey

When you add honey to your CP soap, don't insulate the batch with a blanket as the honey increases the overall batch temperature and cracks and curdles the soap in the moulds. Don't use more than 2 tsp (10 ml) per 2.2 lbs (1 kg) of oils. Add the honey just after trace as its active enzymes are destroyed at temperatures greater than 100.4°F (38°C). It benefits skin as it is an antioxidant, absorbs impurities, and has antimicrobial and anti-ageing properties. Vegans don't use soap made with honey.

Oats (*Avena sativa*)

Use whole, or grind rolled oats to powder and add at trace. You can also make oatmeal milk by soaking oats in hot water or milk. Use this as the water portion of the recipe. Oats has skin-softening properties and is mildly exfoliant. I don't like to add it as a sprinkled topping as it's not completely saturated with soap and is susceptible to weevils over time. Instant oats is NOT suitable for soap making.

Propolis

This is a natural plant glue used by bees. It is sticky and irritating to work with. Combine it with almonds to make it simpler to grind. Grind the combination powders as finely as possible and add a little at trace. It is antibacterial and anti-inflammatory and the texture will provide mild exfoliation.

Aloe gel or juice

Aloe ferox and Aloe vera have excellent wound-healing properties. Use the juice as a liquid in place of the water in the formula. The gel can be added at trace at 1 tsp (5 ml) per 2.2 lbs (1 kg) of oils.

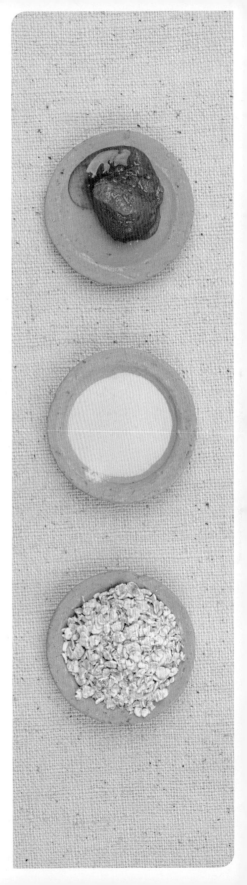

stearin acid

kaolin clay

liquid vegetable glycerine

beeswax

silk

grated processed beeswax

IMPROVE LATHERING, THICKEN OR HARDEN SOAP

Beeswax

Beeswax is used to harden soap bars. Melt it with the oils at no more than .53 oz (15 g) per 2.2 lbs (1 kg) of oils. Use natural beeswax, not synthetic cosmetic versions. Some people may have skin sensitivities to bee products, and they're also not suitable for vegans.

Stearic acid

Make sure you're using the vegetable form, as this is also found in animal tallow. It acts as a hardener for the soap bar. If you're using palm or palm kernel oil for hardness, and you give your soaps enough time to cure (water evaporates and the bar hardens with time), you don't need to add stearic acid. If you do add it, melt it with the oils at 5 tsp (25 ml) per 2.2 lbs (1 kg) of oils.

Liquid vegetable glycerine

Although glycerine will be naturally present in your soap as a result of saponification, you can add extra glycerine at 4 tsp (20 ml) per 2.2 lbs (1 kg) of oils to boost the foaming ability of the soap.

Silk

Silk threads from the cocoons of silkworms can be added to the lye water to dissolve. This gives soap a slightly silky texture. (In my opinion, it's just a gimmick that enables you to call it a silk soap.)

Kaolin clay

This has astringent properties, but can be drying if you use too much. Use at 1–5% and add at early trace.

Bentonite clay

Bentonite clay improves slip in shaving soaps. Use at 1–5% and add at early trace. It will add colour to your bar, but too much will be drying to the skin.

Lecithin

Lecithin's molecular structure is similar to that of soap, with a head and tail, so it acts as a surfactant. It also works as an emulsifier. It comes from egg yolks, soya beans, legumes or brewer's yeast. Add to the oils at 4 tsp (20 ml) per 2.2 lbs (1 kg) of soap.

PRESERVATION

Preservation is optional. Preservatives are added to the oils before the blending process begins. You can avoid using added preservatives by not superfatting your recipe. Superfatting provides a creamier, more moisturising bar, but it means unsaponified oils are present in the bar and can turn rancid with time. Fully saponified soap bars can last for years. I still have my original experiments from 15 years ago, and they are fine.

Superfatted soaps can show DOS – 'dreaded orange spots' in crafting lingo – after a few months if you have not used any preservative.

Soaps containing milks, aloe gel and honey will spoil sooner, so it's advisable to use extra preservatives when using these additives.

SOME NATURAL PRESERVATIVES ARE:

Tocopheryl acetate (vitamin E acetate) is a common vitamin supplement that is high in antioxidants in combination with acetic acid, a component of vinegar. As it is not oxidized it can penetrate the skin and is an ideal preservative. Avoid synthetic versions and use the natural option (vegetable origin). Add 1% to the warmed oils before adding lye.

Grapefruit seed extract is a vitamin C antioxidant – a by-product of the citrus industry – that can extend the shelf life of your superfatted soaps by up to a year. It's expensive and difficult to find. It shortens tracing time, so be prepared. I would only use it for making superfatted soaps on a non-commercial scale. Use at 0.5% concentration and add to warmed oils before adding lye.

Rosemary oleoresin – or **ROE** – is a natural antioxidant, not a preservative, so it won't stop bacterial growth, but it will extend the shelf life of soaps and base oils. It helps prevent oxidation because it contains carnosic acid. Be sure to buy ROE with a high carnosic acid content – upwards of 5%, otherwise it won't be much help in preserving anything.

It has a slight rosemary aroma, but this doesn't carry to the end soap. It will also appear to change your base colour, but this too disappears. Use it at 0.2–0.8% of your batch, adding it to the melted warm oils before you combine the oil and lye.

You can also add the ROE to your bulk stored oils, to preserve their shelf life. It isn't easy to find, but well worth using if you can.

VISUAL EFFECT

Dried flower petals, pressed flowers, tapioca, sago, dried citrus rind, oats, bran, chopped nuts and dried leaves can all be added to the tops of your soaps for visual effect. These need to be added at very thick trace to get them to suspend, or laid in the bottom of the mould – which becomes the top of the bar – and the pour needs to be done very gently and gradually to keep the coating even.

making soap

basic methods

I will briefly discuss four basic methods of soap making and then take you step by step through the cold-process method.

Melt-and-pour method (M&P)

This soap-making method is very simple and won't really be covered in this book. All it means is that you go to a soap-making crafting shop and buy ready-made glycerine or M&P soap rods, which can even be pre-fragranced and pre-coloured for you. You then melt this gently and pour it into moulds, allow them to set and then pop them out. It cannot be simpler. You don't need a book to do this.

To make the rods from scratch is another story entirely, as it requires quite a bit of chemistry and raw materials that are only available in bulk from industrial suppliers. This soap cannot be classed as a natural soap, so it will not be discussed in this book.

Cold process method (CP)

CP or cold process soap making is what you will learn from this book, with supplementary information on our website (www.rainafrica.com). Cold process does not mean that no heat is used (as I once naïvely believed). You will use heat to melt and combine the butters and oils. The lye and water generate heat when combined, and this latent heat is enough to cause saponification (with a few caveats, like keeping it warm enough while it goes through its gel phase). This heat transforms the ingredients into soap. However, the heat is not enough to drop the pH to skin-safe levels, which means the soaps will have to sit on a shelf and cure like cheese for at least four weeks, until the pH drops naturally to around 9–10.5 (see the step-by-step process, page 74).

Cold process oven process (CPOP)

This is a kind of marriage between CP and HP in that you make your soaps in the CP way, and then you place your mould into a warm oven for two hours to speed up the gel phase and induce evaporation. It is, in fact, a hot process method, but done in the oven and not in a slow cooker. One benefit of this method is that it will reduce your curing time. However, it is not suitable for all types of soaps – dairy or honey-based soaps will overheat and curdle.

BENEFITS OF THIS TECHNIQUE:
· Once you have mastered the CP method, this is a very easy next step
· You are unlikely to have partial gelling due to insufficient heat build-up
· Colours are likely to be slightly richer
· Curing time will be shortened by at least a week due to the water evaporation that takes place in the oven with the extra heat
· You can achieve a kind of crackly effect on titanium dioxide, so CPOP is used to obtain special finishing effects

HOW TO DO CPOP:
· Preheat the oven to 158-176°F (70–80°C) (warm setting)
· Make a cold process batch as you normally would
· Pour into your mould (do not cover)
· Place in preheated oven for two hours
· Do not open the oven door
· Turn off the oven and leave the soap mould in the oven overnight as you would for meringues
· Unmould, cut and stack on drying racks to cure further

Hot process method (HP)

This is again a step beyond cold process. You simply make the cold process soap and then cook the batter for a few hours over medium to high heat (in this case in a slow cooker or double boiler), which forces the pH to drop and the soap to neutralise. This eliminates the need for a long curing time and the soap is technically ready for immediate use, but I would still cure the soaps for a further two weeks to really harden and refine the bars. To check that you can, in fact, use it immediately, do a pH test with strips or with phenolphthalein. Add a few drops of phenolphthalein to the soap in the pot and if it turns pink, the soap is still too alkaline for safe use and must be cooked some more.

The major benefit of this method is that your essential oils are added when the soap is neutralised, so their fragile properties are not damaged or lost because of the high alkalinity of the uncured soap batter. This means you can use smaller amounts of essential oil – a big cost saving! The downside of this method is that the soap is thick and lumpy, so you can't use it for fancy, delicate pouring techniques. You may also struggle to get the batter neatly into your moulds and have a smooth, refined finish to your bars – the texture is coarser and can be spongy.

You have to progress to the hot process soap method if you want to achieve translucent and/or liquid soaps – but this is a technique for another book and another day!

So, let's get on with it and start learning the very simple technique of cold process soap making.

step-by-step cold process soap making

You are now equipped and ready for your first batch of all-natural handmade soap. (Still scared? Go to www.rainafrica.com/tutorials and watch the beginner step-by-step video.) Gather all your raw materials and your basic equipment to be fully prepared and prepare your moulds in advance.

My most important message to you is that flopped batches are almost always caused by wrong measurements. Soap ingredients are weighed – even liquid ingredients.

An important concept to understand when you make soap, is that of "trace". You have achieved "trace" when you reach the critical point at which a soap mixture thickens enough to leave a little pathway across its surface when you dribble the liquid from the stick blender or spoon. If it momentarily sits there like a spidery line (a bit like instant pudding), your soap has reached trace. This is a most important stage in the soap-making process. View the soap in good light and at varying angles to be sure that you can see this line forming. Initially you have what is called a thin trace, when the mixture has the consistency of pancake batter. Medium trace is a thicker consistency, almost like cake batter, and heavy trace means you had better get the soap into the moulds quickly. If the consistency is too thin, you may have had what we call false trace and your soap will not set. Experience will help you play with this timing to your advantage.

BASIC ALL-PURPOSE RECIPE

Makes approximately 2.2 lbs (1 kg) of soap and uses easy-to-obtain ingredients:

- 10.6 oz (300 g) coconut oil
- 21.2 oz (600 g) olive oil
- 2.8 oz (80 g) castor oil
- 5 oz (141 g) caustic soda/lye
- 12.4 oz (352 g) distilled water

1. Place a glass mixing jug or plastic bucket onto the scale. Tare the scale so that it reads zero.
2. Don gloves, goggles and face mask, then weigh out and set aside 5 oz (141 g) of caustic soda (sodium hydroxide, NaOH) – accuracy is very important.
3. Place another glass or plastic jug onto scale, make sure the scale reads zero and weigh out the water or liquid portion of your recipe – 12.4 oz (352 g). Set aside.
4. In a well-ventilated room or outside, add caustic soda to the water and stir till the crystals have dissolved. The liquid turns milky, gets hot and starts to steam. Avoid inhaling these fumes. Never add water to caustic soda as it can cause an eruption and burn you. You now have a lye solution that is instantly hot and has to cool before you add it to the oils.
5. Place the thermometer into this container and leave it there until the temperature drops to around 113°F (45°C). While you wait, start on the oils and butters. (You can temporarily remove your gloves, goggles and mask.)

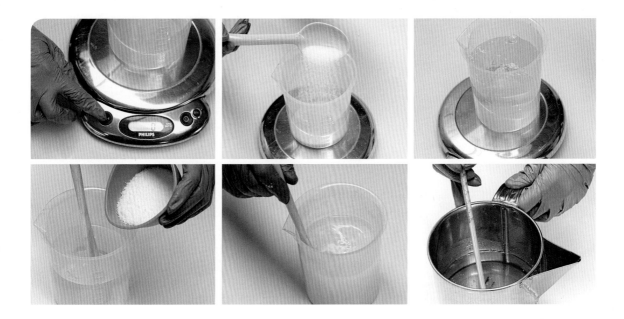

6. Place bowl onto the scale, check that it reads zero, then weigh out the oils and butters in any order – keep a calculator handy to add the weights of each oil as you go, and work with an accumulative total. Otherwise you can weigh each one in a separate dish and add them all to the pot at the end. Put all oil and butter into a stainless steel pot.

7. Weigh or measure out the fragrances, essential oils and additives you wish to use and set aside. Normally these are added after trace, but there are exceptions.

8. Place the pot of oils and butters onto a low heat (or heat in the microwave) to gently but fully melt all the fats together. The oil temperature should be rising to meet the falling temperature of the lye solution. The lye solution and oils should both be around 86-95°F (30–35°C) when you combine them. When the temperatures reach this zone, don your safety goggles, gloves and mask.

9. Using a rubber spatula or wooden spoon, gently pour the lye solution into the oil mixture, stirring all the time until thoroughly combined. Be careful of splashing – this is when you may get lye solution in your eyes.

10. Now take the stick blender, submerge it into the mixture and only then switch it on, otherwise you will splash. Move it around the pot to make sure you get thorough coverage. When the oils no longer rise to the surface and the mixture seems to be one constant colour, the water and oils have emulsified. This stage comes before trace.

11. Continue blending until the soap starts to thicken slightly – you are nearing trace. Slow down the blender so that the soap does not thicken too quickly. Keep checking for signs of trace. Thin trace is good enough for adding colour, then fragrance, and then pouring into moulds. The thinner the trace, the more time you buy to play with fancy techniques (see Special techniques, page 91).

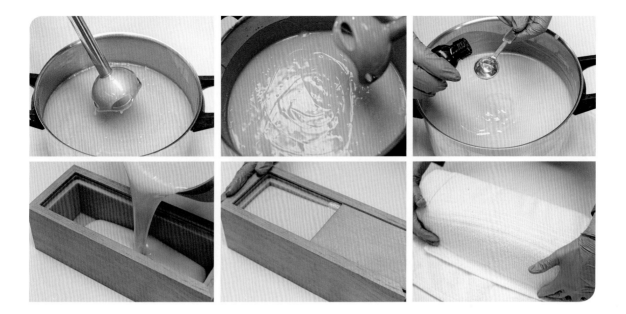

12. Heavy ingredients such as herbs, oats, coffee or seeds, will sink to the bottom of the mould if added at thin trace. Keep blending till you get a thicker trace (a bit like porridge), then add colour, additives, and lastly fragrance. Fragrance or essential oils are left for last as essential oils often accelerate trace, forcing you to get the batter into moulds before colour or additives have made it into the pot.

13. Stir to mix well. You can do a last run with the stick blender to make sure all is well combined.

14. Pour the batter into the mould – keeping your gloves and goggles on. Avoid splashing the mixture as it is still very caustic at this point. Neaten the surface of the soap and wipe away any spills.

15. Sprinkle on a topping if you are using one, or create surface texture with spoon-wave techniques.

16. Cover the mould with a lid, a piece of cardboard, a chopping board or tea tray and wrap with an old towel or blanket to keep warm. Keeping the mixture warm helps the gelling phase take place. The exception to this is honey or milk-based soap – they will curdle with the extra heat.

17. Leave overnight, and with some oil combinations and depending on the weather, 12–24 hours.

18. Remove the blanket and unmould the soap. Measure and cut into slices, or use a special soap or cheese cutter. Trim as required.

19. Stack soap slices onto a drying rack or shelf with good air circulation and leave 4–6 weeks to cure.

20. Use as required or package and label for selling.

some of my own special recipes

Are you interested in making soaps that are beautiful works of art, or are you more interested in the properties that soap can offer your skin? I have tried to please both camps in this book. The Special techniques section (see page 91) will fully satisfy the needs of the creator and artist, and the section to follow is aimed at the soap maker looking for formulas that benefit the skin.

The recipe provided in the Step-by-step cold process soap making section (see page 75) is a safe all-purpose recipe to use in all the special techniques and projects. The recipes in this section are some of my own special favourite formulas – all of them 100% natural. In each case, follow the step-by-step process in the previous section, but substitute the ingredients with those of the chosen recipe.

These recipes are formulated with specific skin benefits in mind and are for everyday use. I have deliberately not been too artistic here in order to differentiate them into a category of their own. They all make roughly a 2.2 lb (1 kg) batch, perfect for home use, made with domestic equipment.

> To upscale the recipes for commercial purposes, estimate what a batch will yield by combining the weight of all the oils. I don't really factor in the lye solution, as evaporation takes place during the curing period and thereafter, and while you never lose all the water you put in, it is more conservative for costing purposes to calculate on the basis of the oils alone. So a 2.2 lb (1 kg) batch will yield roughly 10–12 x 3.5 oz (100 g) soaps. If you've added heavy materials like exfoliants, you can stretch that to another two bars.

To make your own special formulas, the ingredients information in Chapter 2 will be a good start. Use a lye calculator – just add your oil weights and the calculator will adjust the amounts of lye and water required to saponify the oils you have chosen. Several lye calculators are available online:

www.thesage.com/calcs/lyecalc2.php
www.soapcalc.net/calc/soapcalcwp.asp
www.brambleberry.com/pages/Lye-calculator.aspx

ODOUR ABSORBER

Helps with excessive body odour and removes food preparation odours. Here are five variations of odour-absorbing soap:

· Coffee – used by perfumers to neutralise smells in their noses, as it is known for its odour-absorbing properties
· Charcoal – has a high odour-absorbing capability and is often used in fridges to eliminate odours
· Bicarbonate of soda – absorbs odours
· Lemon – a well-known odour absorber
· Alternatively, you can use all of the above in one soap

HOW TO MAKE
1. Use the basic recipe on page 75, but substitute the lye water with leftover filter coffee. Follow the steps for the basic recipe to make the soap.
2. Aim for a thick trace before you add one of the following odour-absorbing materials:
    · 10 tsp (50 ml) used coffee grounds
    · 10 tsp (50 ml) fine charcoal powder (dust) – use a pestle and mortar to pound the charcoal to a fine, lump-free powder
    · 10 tsp (50 ml) finely grated lemon rind and 4 tsp (20 ml) lemon juice
    · 10 tsp (50 ml) bicarbonate of soda
    · 10 tsp (50 ml) of a combination of the above
3. Add the odour-absorbing material into a thick trace just before pouring, to keep the weighty material in suspension. If the mixture is too thin (early trace), the heavier material will fall to the bottom of the mould and not stay evenly distributed. (Perhaps you want it that way, which is also good.)
4. This recipe doesn't really need a fragrance, but you can add one at roughly 2–3% (4-6 tsp (20-30 ml) in this recipe). A coffee fragrance could be nice to enhance the coffee option, or Litsea cubeba essential oil with the lemon version. Eucalyptus goes well with charcoal, and lemongrass with bicarbonate of soda. These are all strong fragrances in themselves, giving the soap double punch.

INSECT REPELLENT

This soap is completely natural and biodegradable – ideal for outdoor activities like hiking and camping. It's a good idea to make fairly small bars as hikers are always watching pack weight. Present it in a small tin so that they can pack the wet soap after use and not have a messy bag.

HOW TO MAKE

1. Use the basic recipe on page 75 and follow the steps to make the soap.
2. Add 4 tsp (20 ml) citronella and 4 tsp (20 ml) lemongrass as insect-repelling essential oils and 1 tsp (5 ml) tea tree essential oil to help heal existing bites, cuts and scrapes.
3. Add 2 tsp (10 ml) turmeric powder for colouring. Place the turmeric into a small bowl and add a tablespoon of the traced soap batter. Using a teaspoon or small spatula, mix to obtain a smooth, lump-free paste. Add a further two tablespoons of soap batter to the paste, mix well, then add the turmeric paste to the main batch of batter and blend with the stick blender.

GARDENER'S SOAP

Choose a mould with botanical connections so that the intent of the soap is clear, and choose herbal or floral essential oils to complement, or some of the interesting perfumes based on vegetable notes, like carrot and celery, green tomato or cucumber. Choose additives like dried herbs or flowers to reinforce the gardening connection. For an exfoliating soap, add something rough to break down the dirt and grime, but also add rich fats and butters to add lost moisture and nourishment to the skin and to repair sun damage. I like to use poppy seeds, ground luffa or rooibos tea for the rougher soap option, and ground dried oats (NOT instant, it will cook and become mush), ground pumice stone or digestive bran for the softer exfoliating options.

INGREDIENTS (SUPERFATTED AT 5%)

- 5.3 oz (150 g) avocado oil
- 2.8 oz (80 g) castor oil
- 9.5 oz (270 g) coconut oil
- 3.5 oz (100 g) jojoba oil
- 8.8 oz (250 g) palm oil
- 2.8 oz (80 g) shea butter
- 2.1 oz (60 g) Kalahari melon oil
- 4.8 oz (135 g) caustic soda/lye
- 12.5 oz (355 g) distilled water

- 4 tsp (20 ml) essential oil – herbal essential oil like rosemary, thyme or sweet basil, or use 6 tsp (30 ml) of a perfume with a gardening theme, like tomato or cucumber.
- For the main exfoliant, choose one of the following: 6 tsp (30 ml) dried chopped luffa; 6 tsp (30 ml) poppy seeds; 4 tsp (20 ml) ground pumice stone; 10 tsp (50 ml) rooibos tea (snip the teabag, sieve through a strainer to take out the very big rough pieces and add); 8 tsp (40 ml) dried finely chopped oats or 8 tsp (40 ml) dried digestive bran

HOW TO MAKE

1. I like to infuse herbs into the liquid (water) as well as into the oils when making a gardening soap. Use either avocado or jojoba oil or both from the ingredients above. Warm the oil to bath-water temperature (not to flash point). Pick culinary herbs from your herb garden, wash them, pat them dry and add them to the warm oil to steep for a day. Strain out the herbs and squeeze, making sure you don't lose any of the oils from your formula. Weigh the oil, and if it has lost any weight through the herbs, add a little to make up the difference. Use the infused oil in place of the plain oil.
2. Heat the distilled water to boiling point and pour it over a selection of washed garden herbs. Allow to steep like tea. When cool, strain out the herbs and make sure your liquid weight is correct for the recipe. If it's short, add a little more plain distilled water to make it up. Use this herbal water infusion to make your lye solution.
3. Proceed as per the step-by-step method on page 75.
4. After trace has been reached, add the fragrance and your choice of exfoliant. You could make a non-exfoliating gardener's soap simply by eliminating the exfoliant and adding dried kitchen herbs instead for a speckled, natural, herbal soap.

RESCUE

This soap has great properties for problem skin owing to its carefully selected oils, which don't exacerbate the oiliness of acne, but bring healing, antibacterial, protective properties.

1. Jojoba is most similar in molecular structure to our own skin's sebum, so it's a highly skin-compatible oil and does not clog pores.
2. Marula oil contains procyanidins that work at scavenging free radicals before they cause damage to cells, and is highly moisturising and conditioning.
3. Rosehip oil is high in gamma-linolenic acid, like hemp seed, but also high in retinol (vitamin A), which helps to fade scarring with use over time.
4. Sunflower oil has natural antioxidants and forms a germ-resistant barrier on the skin.
5. Use reduced levels of coconut oil as it can block pores in high percentages, but it contains lauric acid, which is antibacterial and reduces itching and inflammation.
6. Bentonite clay helps absorb grease and oiliness.
7. Hibiscus extract, also known as the 'botox plant', has highly antioxidant fruit acids – alpha hydroxy acids or AHAs – which exfoliate and speed up cell turnover, control breakouts and improve elasticity and flexibility. It also has astringent properties, reducing the size of the pores.

INGREDIENTS

- 5.3 oz (150 g) sunflower oil
- 2.8 oz (80 g) rosehip oil
- 9.9 oz (280 g) coconut oil
- 3.5 oz (100 g) jojoba oil
- 10.2 oz (290 g) palm oil
- 2.1 oz (60 g) marula or hemp seed oil
- 3 tsp (15 ml) bentonite clay

- 4.7 oz (133 g) caustic soda/lye
- 12.2 oz (345 g) distilled water
- 8.5 TB (125 ml) dried hibiscus flowers (roselle) – found in health shops as a tea
- 2 tsp (10 ml) lavender essential oil
- 2 tsp (10 ml) rosemary essential oil
- 1 tsp (5 ml) tea tree essential oil

HOW TO MAKE

1. Bring the 12.2 oz (345 g) distilled water to the boil and pour it over the hibiscus flowers to make a tea. Allow to steep for a few hours. Strain out the flowers and discard. Keep the water and weigh again, making sure it is 12.2 oz (345 g) (excluding the weight of the container).
2. Follow the step-by-step method on page 75.
3. At trace, take a tablespoon of soap batter and place it in a small bowl with the bentonite clay. Stir to a smooth, lump-free paste.
4. Add the clay-and-batter mix back into the main batch and stir with the stick blender.
5. Add the essential oils and any natural clay colourant you may choose.
6. Pour into the moulds.

NOURISH

This soap, great for very dry or sun-damaged skin, contains:

- sunflower oil, which forms a protective germ-resistant barrier and helps the skin retain water
- shea butter, for intense moisture replenishment
- macadamia nut oil, which reduces redness, irritation and itching
- avocado oil, which soothes sunburn

INGREDIENTS (SUPERFATTED AT 5%)
- 3.5 oz (100 g) macadamia nut oil
- 4.9 oz (140 ml) avocado oil
- 10.6 oz (300 g) coconut oil
- 3.9 oz (110 g) sunflower oil
- 9.5 oz (270 g) palm oil
- 2.8 oz (80 g) shea butter
- 5.1 oz (145 g) caustic soda/lye
- 12.7 oz (359 g) distilled water
- 4 tsp (20 ml) lavender essential oil
- 2 tsp (10 ml) chamomile essential oil

HOW TO MAKE
Follow the step-by-step method on page 75.

ULTRA MILD

This fragrance-free soap is excellent for babies, pregnant moms and people with highly allergic skin. The options for this kind of soap are pure olive oil Castile soap or goat's milk soaps. For now we will stick to the Castile option. Olive oil is highly moisturising and keeps the moisture in without blocking any of the normal functions of the skin like sweating, shedding dead cells and secreting sebum. Remember that olive oil soaps do not lather very well, so don't be disappointed. Also note that pure Castile olive oil soap takes a long time to reach trace. Persevere – it's worth it.

INGREDIENTS
- 2.2 lbs (1 kg) (not extra virgin as it lacks unsaponifiables)
- 4.5 oz (128 g) caustic soda/lye
- 12.7 oz (359 g) distilled water

HOW TO MAKE
1. Simply follow the step-by-step guide on page 75.
2. Fragrance is optional, but if you really want fragrance, use something very mild and safe for pregnancy – like Roman chamomile, geranium or bergamot – and use at 1%, or 2 tsp (10 ml) per 2.2 lb (1 kg) batch.
3. Leave for eight weeks to reduce the pH.

hand milling and rebatching

HAND MILLING

This is the grating down of soap trimmings, offcuts and even less-than-satisfactory batches, and gently reconstituting the gratings with a little liquid over gentle heat or in a double boiler into a thick, mushy medium that can be shaped by hand. You can also hand mill full batches, and not just trimmings and offcuts, but this is an enormous amount of extra work. The benefit of hand milling is that the soap is already saponified, so the high level of caustic activity is gone. This means:

- The essential oils are less likely to be damaged by the intense reactive heat, preserving their special fragile properties.
- Fragrances remain sharp and full, so you need less, and fragrance is an expensive ingredient
- Colours behave more predictably.
- Herbs and seeds remain in suspension instead of falling to the bottom during the gelling phase.
- You have far more control of the outcome.

The longer you leave offcuts and scraps to dry, the more work it is to hand mill them. I prefer to use them as soon as possible after trimming, while they're still soft – then the process requires less effort, liquid and time. The soap is still uncured at this stage and is highly alkaline, so use surgical gloves to protect your hands from drying out.

There are no hard-and-fast rules about amounts of liquid, timing and level of heat. But hand milling also can't really flop. Add more water if you really need to, but don't be in a hurry to do so. Rather use more time and gentle heat to soften the batter. The more water you add, the longer your soaps will take to unmould and dry on the rack. They will also shrink a lot if you've added too much water.

How to hand mill

Grate offcuts with a cheese grater or a meat mincer – wear surgical gloves. There are three methods of working the gratings, all using the same ingredients:

- 2.2 lbs (1 kg) soap gratings
- 6.8 TB (100 ml) water, milk or liquid tea infusions, depending on how dry the gratings are – use as little liquid as possible
- 2 tsp (10 ml) essential oil or fragrance
- A few drops of extra colour if desired

STOVE-TOP METHOD
(size of batch is limited only by the size of the double boiler)

Place gratings and liquid in a double boiler. Cover and warm gently over a low heat, stirring occasionally to mix soap batter and water fully and disperse the heat. Don't over-stir. Melting the mixture gradually takes time and little movement. Allow 10–20 minutes. The double boiler will prevent burning. Add fragrance and colour when the mixture has softened and become cohesive like a chunky batter. Do this by transferring a few tablespoons of the batter into a small bowl, add colour and fragrance to this and mix well. Return to the main mixture, combining well. Scrape the batter into a mould. Pound down with a wooden spoon to release any air pockets. Smooth the surface as best you can. Allow to cool and set overnight, then unmould and cut.

The batter will not be smooth and pourable like newly traced soap, but if you get it as smooth as possible in the double boiler and then smooth down the batter in the moulds as best you can, the end bars look fine.

Instead of pushing the mushy mixture into a mould, you can rework it into balls, egg shapes, ovals or pebble shapes when the batter has cooled a little.

tip: Colours behave differently when soap is reworked like this. The soap is saponified and not an intensely caustic mixture, so colours and fragrance are more stable when added at this stage. Ensure that they disperse evenly in the thick, clumpy medium.

MICROWAVE METHOD
(size of batch is generally 2.2 lbs (1 kg) and fits into most microwaves)

Place gratings and liquid in a microwaveable jug or bowl. Stir minimally to combine. Cover with plastic wrap. Set the heat on medium/high and the timer on 1 minute. After 1 minute, open and stir gently. Repeat this process till the mix becomes slightly translucent. Be careful – it gets hot. Once you're satisfied that it's an integrated, gloopy batter, let it cool marginally before adding fragrance and colour. Stir to incorporate and then scrape the batter into a mould. Pound down with a wooden spoon to release any air pockets. Smooth the surface as best you can. Allow to cool and set overnight, then unmould and cut.

SLOW COOKER/CROCKPOT METHOD
(size of batch is limited only by the size of slow cooker)

tip: You may need more water if the soap is hard and well cured.

Turn the slow cooker on to the highest heat setting. Add the water and colour, then the grated soap. Immediately turn it down to the lowest heat, cover and allow the gratings to melt gently and absorb the liquid. Stir every 5–10 minutes. When the batter has softened and become slightly translucent, turn off the heat and add fragrance and colour, combining well. Scrape the batter into a mould. Pound down with a wooden spoon to release any air pockets. Smooth the surface as best you can. Allow to cool and set overnight, then unmould and cut.

Curing

If you've reworked already cured soap, dry the milled soaps for a few days to a week before use. If you have reworked uncured newly trimmed soaps, cure the hand milled soaps for the normal 4–6 weeks.

REBATCHING

This is the reprocessing of soaps that did not turn out so well – flops, which can be sliced, cubed or cut into sticks to embed into another full batch of soap to create specific patterns.

I love rebatching as an option to make use of flops and trimmings. The results are always superb, interesting and different. Store your soap offcuts in brown paper bags to allow them to breathe – label them in colour groupings so that you can find the right colour palette when you need it. Rebatch only batches that flopped superficially – disappointing colour, fragrance, shape, texture or design. Soap that flopped in terms of wonky chemistry (watery, separated, seized, lye-heavy, etc.) is considered unsafe and should be discarded.

Cut your offcuts into cubes, slices, rods or use cookie cutters to make shapes with them. Position these pieces into loaf moulds and make soap that will need to be sliced (or you won't see the effect of the inserts). These make the best soap designs.

(4)

special soap-making techniques

Do you want to have some serious fun? Then this is it!

These step-by-step techniques are so easy, and they're an avenue for immense creativity. The thrill lies in the unpredictable outcome, and there is a sense of anticipation when you unwrap your mould 24 hours after pouring, and discover what you've created.

To make these recipes, simply use the basic soap recipe on page 75. You can make these projects using your own recipes and special additives, but first get some practise with this basic inexpensive recipe. The steps are demonstrated in our DIY tutorials on our YouTube channel, accessed via www.rainafrica.com/tutorials

Follow the basic step-by-step procedure on page 75 to get the soap batter to trace. Always start off with a light trace, as these techniques often take time to pour and the thicker your trace is, the less time you have to play. Some techniques will need a medium or even a strong trace as you may have to spoon the batter rather than pour it. With practice, you'll learn which viscosity of traced batter works best for which situation.

Prepare well for these techniques. Have all your tools ready, and have your colours and fragrances pre-measured. Have extra cloths, spatulas, jugs and teaspoons – you don't want to be scurrying around trying to find something while your soap is thickening and becoming unpourable.

All these techniques can be done with colours and fragrances of your choice. Make sure you wrap your soap up warmly and don't be tempted to peep for at least 12–24 hours.

I have categorised each technique as follows:
Easy – so simple it's unlikely to flop; little time pressure
Moderate – some skill and practice required; some time pressure
Challenging – may consist of multiple phases requiring a few days to complete, and may involve extreme time pressure or creativity

general instructions

- For every technique mentioned below, you can use the basic recipe on page 75 or your own favourite recipe.
- Prepare bowls with raw colours beforehand, ready to blend with the traced batter. Virtually every technique makes use of natural (uncoloured) soap batter and white or black. The white and black are essential to produce tints and shades, so you'll use them all the time.
- To make white, I use titanium dioxide (the oil-soluble version), blended into a little olive oil till lump-free. This I keep ready to use in a glass screw-cap bottle. To make black, I use purple grass powder. You can also use synthetic black.
- Whenever you add colour, place a spoonful of traced batter into the small bowl of pre-measured colour, blend well with a plastic spoon or a milk frother to ensure the colour is well blended and

lump-free, then add the coloured batter back to the main batch (or to the various jugs of divided batter as instructed) and blend again as illustrated on page 92.

- Follow the step-by-step instructions on page 75 until you reach **light** trace.
- Divide the batter into the specified number of jugs mentioned in each project, and add the small spoonfuls of batter to blend your colours.
- Add fragrance to each jug of colour just before you start the technique, to delay trace reaction resulting from the addition of the fragrance.
- Follow the method mentioned for each specific technique.
- After completing the technique, cover your soap well to insulate it and leave overnight. I call this 'putting your soap to bed'.
- Unwrap the insulation after at least 18 hours, unmould and cut.

A NOTE ABOUT CUTTING AND TRIMMING

You can achieve at least three different effects from a soap technique simply by cutting the finished bars along different planes. You can cut the loaf vertically along the short side, vertically along the long side, or horizontally. In most projects I have done this to show the different effects you get when you cut bars along different planes.

Trim and clean the individual soaps, place on stacking trays with good air circulation and allow to cure for four weeks. To get rid of the powdery white ash, spritz the soap with alcohol before or after unmoulding. To trim the corners, use a knife, a potato peeler of a fairly coarse face cloth as shown.

projects using special techniques

STRIPES

Rating: Moderate

EXTRA EQUIPMENT NEEDED
- Loaf mould
- You need to make divisions in your loaf mould. I have a mould from Taiwan, with perspex dividers, which can be ordered online from Aroma Greens. Alternatively, you can make tight-fitting cardboard divisions, which you can coat with plastic wrap and use a few times before discarding
- Extra jugs – you need one per colour. In this case, I used four

Time to complete: 1 day

Colours: You can use any number of colours. Why not draw inspiration from a Paul Smith tie? I have used four colours here – white, natural ivory (uncoloured), pale grey using charcoal as a colourant, and a synthetic pink colour (Impatiens Pink) from Bramble Berry.

Fragrance: As this soap already has one synthetic colour and can't accurately be classified as natural, I was willing to use a synthetic perfume (I chose a watermelon fragrance) just for fun – 5 tsp (25 ml) was enough for this batch.

METHOD
1. Prepare your mould with equally spaced parallel divisions. Make sure these divisions fit very tightly to avoid leakage underneath the rows.
2. Bring soap to a light trace.
3. Divide the batter equally among four jugs. Leave one jug natural, with no colour. One jug gets 2 tsp (10 ml) charcoal, one gets 1 tsp (5 ml) oil-soluble titanium dioxide (pre-diluted) to make it white, and one gets a few drops of Impatiens Pink. Add pink a little at a time until you like the shade.
4. Now pour a row of each colour. Keep a steady hand so as not to spill over into the next division.
5. When the pouring is done, gently lift the divisions, allowing the soap stripes to merge slightly.
6. Stamp the mould down to remove any air pockets that may be left from the removal of the divisions.
7. Put to bed.
8. Unmould 24 hours later. Cut the loaf in half. With one half, cut soaps lengthwise, and with the other half, cut soaps widthwise. You will achieve two very different effects.

MULTIPLE FUNNEL TECHNIQUE

Rating: Moderate

EXTRA EQUIPMENT NEEDED
- Funnels – I used four, but you can use two, three or even five
- Cardboard top with holes cut to hold the funnels in place while you're pouring
- Extra jugs to match the number of colours you're using
- Little bowls for colour and teaspoons for blending

Time to complete: 1 day

Colours: You can use any number of colours – I used one per funnel. In this project I chose to use various natural clays and powdered seaweed (spirulina powder). Their natural colours were tints and shades of green, which gives a very soothing effect. Choosing stronger contrasting colours will give a much more striking effect using this technique. I used five colour variations here: natural (uncoloured), white (with titanium dioxide), bentonite clay, spirulina powder and French green clay. Aim for two light and two dark ones.

Fragrance: This all-natural clay soap demanded an all-natural green essential oil blend of 3 tsp (15 ml) spearmint and 1 tsp (5 ml) rosemary.

METHOD
1. Prepare your mould with a simple cardboard top with holes for the funnels.
2. Bring soap to a light trace.
3. Divide the batter equally among five jugs. Leave one jug natural, and mix one with 1 tsp (5 ml) oil-soluble titanium dioxide, two with one tablespoon each of the clays mentioned above and one with 2-4 tsp (10-20 ml) of the spirulina powder. Make sure your colours are visibly different in tonal strength – too subtle a shade difference and you won't see any effect.
4. Add essential oil to all the jugs and stir.
5. Now randomly pour from each jug into any funnel, a little at a time. The smaller the pours, the more interesting the results. Random is the key in this technique. The pattern is formed by the pools of colour merging.
6. When the batter is finished, gently lift off the cardboard cover housing the funnels.
7. Stamp the mould down to remove air bubbles.
8. Put to bed.
9. When you unmould the soap the following day, cut the soap in various directions (vertically, horizontally or along the large surface side). This will produce different pattern results.

TRICOLOUR

Rating: Challenging

EXTRA EQUIPMENT NEEDED
- Loaf mould
- One jug per colour
- Chopstick

Time to complete: 1 day

Colours: Use a dark, a light and an accent colour – my accent colour is a russet ochre.

Fragrance: For this all-natural soap I used a woody blend of 3 tsp (15 ml) palmarosa and 1 tsp (5 ml) cedarwood.

METHOD
1. The key to this technique is to have no distractions and complete concentration. You need to pour two jugs at the same time, **very** steadily and at exactly the same speed.
2. Divide batter into three parts. The third jug (the accent colour) can have a little less than the light and dark colour jugs. Add fragrance across all the jugs and stir in.
3. My light colour was left natural and uncoloured. My dark colour had two tablespoons of cocoa blended into it to get a rich, dark, chocolate colour. The accent jug had around 4 tsp (20 ml) of Brazilian red clay blended into it.
4. Take the light and dark batter jugs in different hands. Aim their spouts at the centre and along the inner edge of the mould. Pour simultaneously, very gently and at the same speed. Don't stop. Keep the speed of flow from both jugs the same.
5. Your batter will form a very straight, neat dividing line down the middle of the mould which it will only maintain as long as your pouring speeds do not alter.
6. When the two jugs are empty, take the third jug of accent colour and pour it very gently from a low height along the middle of the joining line, as neatly as possible.
7. Take a thick chopstick and, beginning at a corner, pull the chopstick into horseshoe shapes along the short side all the way down the mould (see diagram on p. 168).

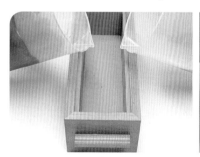  

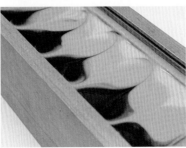
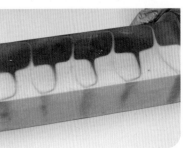

PILLAR EMBEDS

Rating: Challenging

EXTRA EQUIPMENT NEEDED

- Different sized tubes – I bought a set of round plastic pastry cutters (concentric circles) from a baking shop
- Packaging tape
- Loaf mould
- One jug per colour

Time to complete: 2 days

Colours: For the most visually interesting effects with this technique, you need to choose a colour palette, and then make as many possible variations in tint, shade and tone around that theme. I chose Brazilian red clay, Brazilian pink clay, white and natural. My main pour was made using a medium shade of cocoa powder.

Fragrance: The soap is so visually stimulating that I went with simple vanilla oil as a fragrance – I added 8 tsp (40 ml) as this mould was large.

METHOD

1. First tape up one side of the cookie cutters to create various sized small pillar moulds. Choose smaller pillars if your mould is narrow.
2. Make a quarter batch of soap to fill these moulds.
3. Pour each one differently – some swirled, some half-and-half, some striped.
4. Allow to set overnight. Unmould.
5. Place these pillars randomly into your main mould.
6. Make a full batch of soap to pour in between the pillars. Make the colour either lighter or darker than your pillar variations to show them off. I used cocoa powder to get a dark, rich tone.
7. When you cut the hardened soap, you can achieve two strikingly different designs – a horizontal cut showcases the roundness of the pillars and you get polka dots, whereas a vertical cut gives a retro look, showing squares.

 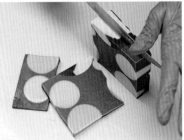 

SHAPE EMBEDS

Rating: Easy

EXTRA EQUIPMENT NEEDED
- Cookie cutters – two different sizes to allow for a ring to be poured
- A fish-shaped mould

Time to complete: 2 days

Colours: The fish were made from white batter with a few drops of light blue colour. The hoops were white batter, and the main base was a slightly darker shade of blue.

Fragrance: 5 tsp (25 ml) of an oceanic ozonic fragrance.

METHOD
1. Make the fish and hoops the day before. The fish are simply poured into a fish-shaped mould. The hoops are poured between two cookie cutters of different sizes.
2. When hardened, embed them into the soap that has been poured into individual moulds. The soap batter should be well traced and thickening so that the shapes don't fall over. The thicker batter also allows it to be piled up around the embedded shapes to create some dimension.

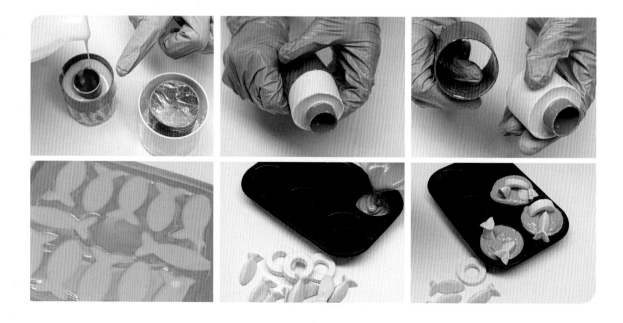

CUT-OUTS

Rating: Easy

EXTRA EQUIPMENT NEEDED
- Shaped cookie cutters
- Individual silicone moulds

Time to complete: 2 days

Colours: I used white, lilac and purple.

Fragrance: 4 tsp (20 ml) lavender essential oil.

METHOD
1. This project is ideal for rebatching – using flopped soaps for your cut-outs, or making your cut-outs from excess batter pours on previous projects.
2. I had extra batter when I made the Slice embed project (see page 106), so I poured some individual moulds with the coloured soap batter from that project.
3. As the Slice embed project had used lavender fragrance, I stuck to the same for this one.
4. Use any cookie cutters you have – choose a shape that fits your soap.
5. Cut out shapes and lay them into individual mould pans.
6. Pour a plain colour around them, taking care to keep the shape of the cut-out clearly visible and making sure that the pour is at the same height as your cut-out.

SLICE EMBEDS

Rating: Challenging

EXTRA EQUIPMENT NEEDED
- Triangle mould on a stand, made out of cardboard and covered with plastic wrap
- Sharp knife
- Pre-made polka dot soaps (see page 129), sliced thinly

Time to complete: 2 days

Colours: Three shades of purple, from light to very dark, and white. My synthetic turquoise colour delivers this purple in a finished soap!

Fragrance: 4 tsp (20 ml) lavender essential oil.

METHOD
1. Separate batter into four jugs – make one white with 1 tsp (5 ml) titanium dioxide, one pale purple with .6 tsp (3 ml) colour, one with 1.2 tsp (6 ml) colour and one with 1.8 tsp (9 ml) colour.
2. Follow the technique for Polka Dots (see page 129).
3. Harden overnight. Remove from mould and slice thinly – thinly enough to allow the soap to curve and bend.
4. Make two cardboard triangle-shaped moulds. Line with plastic wrap.
5. In one mould, place the slices vertically along the middle of the mould.
6. In the other mould, place the slices flat along the walls of the mould.
7. Pour in a batch of white batter, keeping slices apart from one another in mould one and keeping them flat against the walls in mould two.
8. Put to bed. Unmould and cut to reveal two different effects.

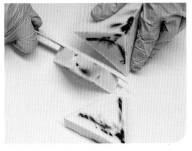

BASIC SWIRL

Rating: Easy

EXTRA EQUIPMENT NEEDED
- One jug per colour
- Loaf mould
- Chopstick

Time to complete: 1 day

Colours: I used two colours – grey Canadian glacial mud and indigo blue powder – and natural batter.

Fragrance: 4 tsp (20 ml) jasmine essential oil.

METHOD
1. Measure out three jugs, keeping one natural and colouring the other two in shades of the chosen colour.
2. Taking the lightest and darkest colour jugs, one in each hand, aim them at the middle of the mould.
3. Pour slowly and simultaneously, taking care to keep the speed of pour the same.
4. The soap will form its own dividing line down the middle.
5. Take the third jug and pour it (from high up) down the middle of the line. The height of the pour causes a natural internal swirl in the soap.
6. Draw a chopstick through the mould – vertically or horizontally, as you prefer (see diagram on p. 168).

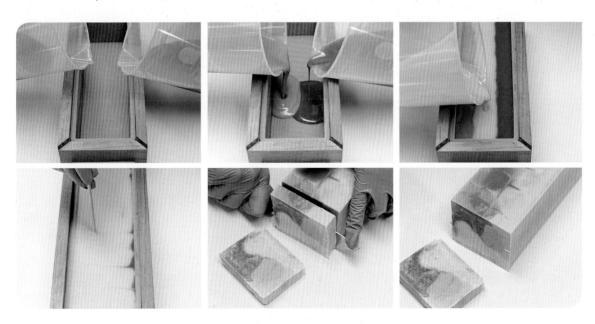

FUNNEL-AND-PIPE TECHNIQUE

Rating: Easy

EXTRA EQUIPMENT NEEDED

- Pringles chips can (for this batch, you'll need 2–3 cans – they cannot be reused)
- A piece of garden hose the length of the Pringles can
- A kitchen funnel
- One jug per colour
- Packaging tape

Time to complete: 1 day

Colours: I used a yellow mica powder, charcoal powder and white.

Fragrance: 4 tsp (20 ml) *Litsea cubeba* essential oil.

METHOD

1. Divide batter into three. Colour one white with 1 tsp (5 ml) titanium dioxide, colour one with 1 tsp (5 ml) yellow mica pre-blended with a little olive oil, and one with 2 tsp (10 ml) charcoal powder.
2. Cut off the metal base of the Pringles can; replace with the plastic lid, taped securely to the core.
3. Attach a small length of hosepipe to a kitchen funnel and place it into the Pringles can.
4. Pour each colour of batter into the Pringles can, in random order and random amounts – start with a little of each, then a lot of one and a little of the other two, etc. Fill the can and put to bed.
5. When hard, cut or pull off the can– the strip unravels itself as you start pulling at the top.

STICKS IN A BOTTLE

Rating: Easy

EXTRA EQUIPMENT NEEDED
· Moulds to make rods, like small candy tubes, or even large fat drinking straws for smoothies. I used an ice tray found in a kitchen shop
· Plastic household cleaner bottle with top cut off to the length of the rods

Time to complete: 2 days

Colours: I used a pale pink Brazilian clay with white and natural batter.

Fragrance: 4 tsp (20 ml) neroli essential oil.

METHOD
1. Pour the sticks/rods using your rod mould, making them in white and pale pink.
2. Cut the neck off a plastic household cleaning bottle to the length of the rods (I cut mine too short in this demonstration!).
3. Bundle rods together randomly and hold with elastic band.
4. Place in the bottle and pour natural batter around them.
5. Stamp down the mould, making sure you get rid of any air bubbles.
6. Release the elastic once the soap thickens, then put to bed.
7. The bottle will need to be cut off the soap and will not be reusable.

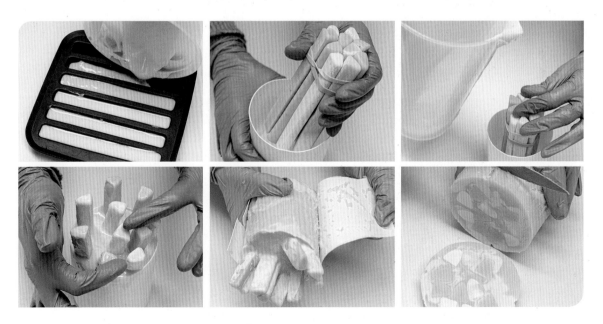

BASIC DIAGONAL SWIRL

Rating: Easy

EXTRA EQUIPMENT NEEDED
- Cardboard divider measured to fit mould diagonally
- Loaf mould
- Chopstick

Time to complete: 1 day

Colours: Natural and mangosteen fruit powder.

Fragrance: 4 tsp (20 ml) cedarwood essential oil.

METHOD
1. Place the diagonal divider into the mould so that it fits very tightly to avoid leakage at the bottom.
2. Divide your batter in two – one natural and one with 4 tsp (20 ml) mangosteen fruit powder or any other colour.
3. Pour one colour into one cavity and the other into the remaining cavity
4. Gently remove the divider.
5. Using a thick chopstick, swirl in a looping fashion (see diagram on p. 168).

PATTERN IMPRINTS – LACE

Rating: Easy

EXTRA EQUIPMENT NEEDED
- Patterned, embossed surfaces on which to pour, like silicone mats used for chocolate making
- Cardboard and packaging tape

Time to complete: 1 day

Colour: White or natural.

Fragrance: 4 tsp (20 ml) of an elegant, feminine fragrance like ylang ylang.

METHOD
1. Make a cardboard mould to fit the embossed surface and the height of the finished soaps (I used silicone mats bought at a baking shop).
2. Cover the cardboard mould with packaging tape or plastic wrap to make it easy to remove the soap, and to make it reusable.
3. Pour the fragranced batter onto the mat.
4. Put to bed.
5. Unmould and peel off the silicone mat.

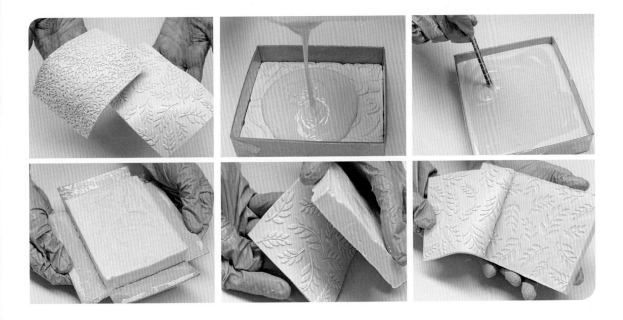

VEINS – VERSION ONE: MUSHROOM

Rating: Moderate

EXTRA EQUIPMENT NEEDED
- Loaf mould
- Small, fine-meshed tea strainer
- Deep plastic teaspoons
- Skewer stick

Time to complete: 1 day

Colours: White, natural and red yeast rice powder for the mushroom colour, mink mica.

Fragrance: You need time to work on this technique, so avoid a floral fragrance that will accelerate trace. I used 4 tsp (20 ml) spearmint essential oil.

METHOD
1. Divide the batter into three and colour.
2. Pour natural batter into the bottom of the mould.
3. Place spoonfuls of the mushroom colour on top of the base layer, taking care not to break through – but only along one side of the pan.
4. Place a teaspoonful of mink mica into the mesh strainer and lightly dust the soap area next to the spooned mushroom. Make sure it is well covered.
5. Then spoon white batter gently on top of the mica powder and, next to it, spoon a layer of natural batter.
6. Dust mica powder over the half that did not previously get dusted.
7. Fill mould with remaining batter.
8. Dust top with remaining mica and make a shallow mini-swirl on the top with a skewer stick.

VEINS – VERSION TWO: CLOUD NINE

Rating: Moderate

EXTRA EQUIPMENT NEEDED
- Loaf mould
- Small fine-meshed tea strainer
- Deep plastic teaspoons

Time to complete: 1 day

Colours: White, pale blue and gold mica dust.

Fragrance: You need time for this technique, so avoid a floral fragrance that will accelerate trace. I used 4 tsp (20 ml) patchouli essential oil.

METHOD
1. Colour half the batter blue, the other half white. Pour blue batter into the bottom of the mould.
2. Place a teaspoonful of gold mica dust into the mesh strainer and dust half of the soap.
3. Spoon white batter gently over the whole area, taking care not to break through to the layers beneath.
4. Place some more blue over the sections.
5. Dust the opposite half with gold mica dust, covering well.
6. Top the whole area with blue again.
7. Spoon the white randomly along the top, allowing blue to show.

SPOON LAYERING

Rating: Easy

EXTRA EQUIPMENT NEEDED
- Loaf mould
- Large plastic spoons, one per colour

Time to complete: 1 day

Colours: This technique works best with a white or natural and one other strong colour, like pink, blue, black or orange. In this case I used white and yellow.

Fragrance: 4 tsp (20 ml) mandarin essential oil.

METHOD
1. The only trick with this technique is patience and a thickly traced batter. Thin batter means the spoonfuls might break through to the lower layer. You also need the batter to maintain its spoon shape when you put it down.
2. Work quickly, as your batter is already well traced, but keep going – one spoonful of each colour at a time.
3. Try to build up a tower structure on the sides of the mould – spooning up the sides so that the end result looks like a skateboard ramp. Then fill up the valleys with the contrasting colour.

COLUMN POUR – TRIANGLE

Rating: Easy

EXTRA EQUIPMENT NEEDED
- Cardboard triangle column – put sand in it for weight, then cover with plastic wrap.
- Mould – I used a Pringles can, but you can use a gutter downpipe or any other mould.

Time to complete: 1 day

Colours: I used chromium oxide green in two strengths (1 tsp [5 ml] and 2 tsp [10 ml]), and a white batter.

Fragrance: 4 tsp (20 ml) rosemary essential oil.

METHOD
1. Place triangle in the mould.
2. Divide batter into three – two shades of green and one white.
3. Aim the spout of the first jug at the middle of the top of the triangle shape and pour gently, allowing the soap to flow down the main sides of the triangle, alternating colours.
4. Fill the mould and gently remove the column.
5. If you have a large column in a small mould, like I have, you will have a big void when you remove the mould, so your soap will subside to half the height of the mould.
6. Cut or pull off the Pringles-tin. It unravels when you start pulling it at the top.

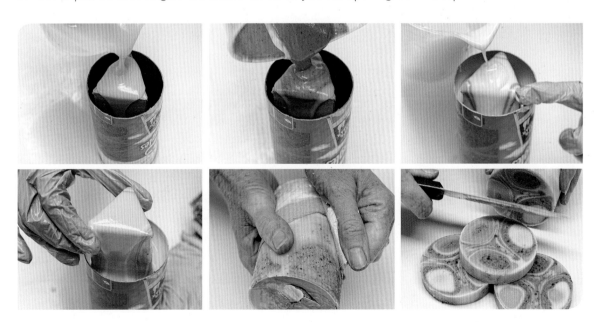

COLUMN POUR – SQUARE

Rating: Easy

EXTRA EQUIPMENT NEEDED
· Mould
· Cardboard column weighed down with sand and covered with plastic wrap, or a square wooden block

Time to complete: 1 day

Colours: I used white, Australian dark red clay, Canadian glacial mud and charcoal.

Fragrance: 4 tsp (20 ml) palmarosa essential oil.

METHOD
1. Place square column into the middle of the mould at an angle to the corners.
2. Divide batter into four – two shades of grey from 1 tsp (5 ml) mud and 2 tsp (10 ml) charcoal, white, and dark red Australian clay at 2 tsp (10 ml).
3. Aim the spout of the first jug (red) at the middle of the top of the column and pour gently, allowing the soap to flow down the main sides of the column, alternating colours.
4. Fill the mould and gently remove the column. The soap will close up neatly by itself.
5. Put to bed.
6. Unmould and see the various pattern options you can get by the different angles of the cut.

POLKA DOTS

Rating: Easy

EXTRA EQUIPMENT NEEDED
- Individual silicone moulds

Time to complete: 1 day

Colours: I used yellow mica, charcoal and white.

Fragrance: 4 tsp (20 ml) lemon essential oil.

METHOD
1. Divide batter into three equal jugs.
2. Colour one jug white with 2 tsp (10 ml) titanium dioxide to get a very white batch, one jug yellow with 1 tsp (5 ml) yellow mica (pre-blended with a spot of olive oil or glycerine) and one jug with 1 tsp (5 ml) charcoal.
3. It doesn't matter in what order you pour the colours – each can be different.
4. Pour one colour, then a second, aiming into the middle of the mould and stopping before the flow reaches the sides.
5. Keep doing this, creating a kind of target effect.

MINESHAFT – WITH SWIRL

Rating: Challenging

EXTRA EQUIPMENT NEEDED

- Mould
- Pliers
- Some shapes to create your mineshaft – I used straight-sided egg cups

Time to complete: 2 days

Colours: The main mine section is natural soap batter, the swirl uses Bramble Berry Lemon Neon and Pool Blue.

Fragrance: 4 tsp (20 ml) vanilla.

METHOD

1. Place egg cups into the mould, leaving enough space between each other and mould sides to create thick enough walls.
2. Pour the fragranced natural batter to fill the mould.
3. Leave overnight. Remove the egg cups, using pliers.
4. Then prepare the two colours. These will use a small amount of batter from the whole soap batch, so best do this project in conjunction with another, or make only a quarter batch of soap to fill the mineshafts.
5. Pour in the blue and then, from height, pour in the yellow. The height causes a mini in-the-jug swirl effect (see page 150). Fill the mineshafts.

MINESHAFT – WITH STRIPES

Rating: Challenging

EXTRA EQUIPMENT NEEDED
- Mould
- Some shapes to create your mineshaft. I used straight-sided egg cups and also small squeeze bottles, filled with water to weigh them down.
- Pliers

Time to complete: 2 days

Colours: The main mine section is natural soap batter, then I used five different colours of natural clay, and cocoa powder for the very dark stripe (.41 tsp [2 ml] of each, as it takes only a small batch to fill the mineshafts).

Fragrance: 4 tsp (20 ml) sandalwood essential oil.

METHOD
1. Place bottles into the mould and fill the bottom of the mould with fragranced natural batter.
2. Add the egg cups, leaving enough space between cups, bottles and the mould sides for reasonably thick walls, and fill the moulds.
3. Leave overnight. Remove egg cups and bottles using pliers.
4. Then prepare the various colours. These will use a small amount of batter from the whole soap batch, so best do this project in conjunction with another, or make only a quarter batch of soap to fill the mineshafts.
5. Pour in the first layer with a jug. The next layers have to be added by spoon to avoid breaking through to the layer below. Alternate randomly until mineshafts are full.
6. Pour your leftover soap in random order to fill up your mould to the rim, or mix all leftovers together in a jug and fill mould.

PAINT-AND-PIPE MICA

Rating: Moderate

EXTRA EQUIPMENT NEEDED:
- Ziplock bag
- Paintbrushes – 1 for each colour mica used
- Empty glass jug
- Scissors
- Individual moulds

Time to complete: 1 day

Colours: I used a white and a bronze mica.

Fragrance: 4 tsp (20 ml) rose essential oil.

METHOD
1. Blend mica powder with a little glycerine or olive oil. Make sure the paste is lump-free.
2. With a paintbrush, randomly brush the insides of the ziplock bag with both colours of mica (random is the key).
3. Put the bag into a jug for support and fill it with fragranced natural batter.
4. Close the zip and make sure it is well sealed.
5. Snip off the corner of the bag to pipe the batter into the moulds. The mica colour is picked up by the batter as it moves along.

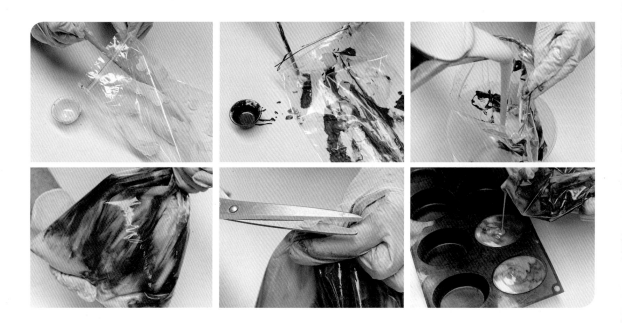

SUSPENDED CIRCLE

Rating: Challenging

EXTRA EQUIPMENT NEEDED
- A tube mould (like a candy tube) at least the full length of your mould as it must fit tightly against the walls of the mould
- Mould – to complement length of tube

Time to complete: 2 days

Colours: I used white and charcoal.

Fragrance: 4 tsp (20 ml) blend of basil, lime and mint essential oils.

METHOD
1. Make a quarter batch of soap or make this project when you're doing another project as it will not use a lot of soap batter.
2. Make the batter half white and half dark charcoal. Add one to the other causing an in-the-jug swirl (see page 150). Pour this into the tube and allow to harden overnight.
3. Again make a batch of white and black – I used purple grass powder for this.
4. Pour a layer of white, filling half the mould.
5. Jam the tube into the middle of the mould to suspend it and keep it from sinking.
6. Fill the second half of the mould with black batter.

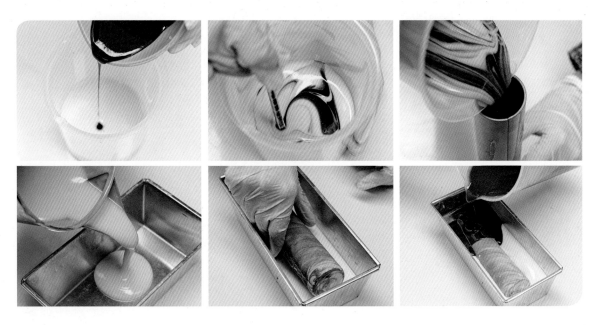

COAT-HANGER SWIRL – PARTIAL DEPTH

Rating: Easy

EXTRA EQUIPMENT NEEDED
- Old coat hanger bent into a squared-off U-shape to fit your mould
- Thick drinking straw to place over the bottom of the hanger wire – optional (for a broader effect)
- Loaf mould

Time to complete: 1 day

Colours: White and black.

Fragrance: 5 tsp (25 ml) coconut fragrance.

METHOD
1. Divide batter into two – two-thirds for white and one-third for black.
2. Fill half the mould with white batter.
3. Gently spoon on all the black batter – don't break through to the next layer.
4. Spoon on the remaining white layer.
5. Now insert the bent coathanger only halfway down the depth of the mould.
6. Move from one side of the mould to the other with a U-movement, bringing black from the middle up into the white section (see diagram on p. 168).
7. Do not go lower than half of the mould height.

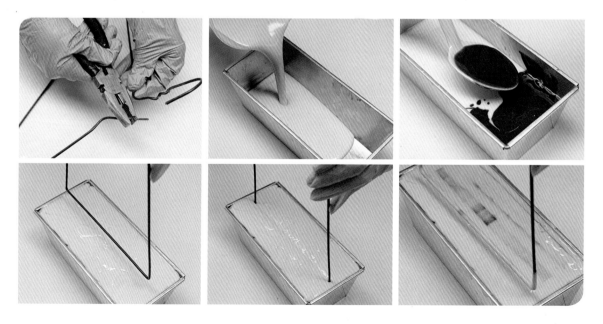

COAT-HANGER SWIRL – LOOPING SWIRL

Rating: Easy

EXTRA EQUIPMENT NEEDED

- Old coat hanger bent into a squared-off U-shape to fit your mould
- Loaf mould
- Thick drinking straw to place over the bottom of the hanger wire – optional (for a broader effect)
- Tea strainer
- Spatula or chopstick

Time to complete: 1 day

Colours: I used black, natural and mustard mica pre-blended with olive oil.

Fragrance: 4 tsp (20 ml) bergamot essential oil.

METHOD

1. Divide batter into three – half for natural, one-quarter for mustard mica and one-quarter for black.
2. Fill half the mould with natural batter, reserving half for the top.
3. Gently spoon on all the black so as not to break through to the next layer.
4. Spoon on the mustard mica – gently, so as not to break through.
5. Spoon on the balance of the natural batter to fill mould.
6. Now insert the bent coat hanger only halfway down the depth of the mould, leaving the first pour of natural undisturbed.
7. With a looping swirl movement, you'll bring black and mustard mica into the top layer of natural (see diagram on p. 168).
8. Place a little mica powder into a tea strainer or small sieve and gently dust the top of the loaf with a light sprinkeling of the sparkly mica.
9. Create a swirl effect on the top only with your spatula or chopstick, taking care not to penetrate more than .04 inch (1 mm).

SPIDERWEB

Rating: Moderate

EXTRA EQUIPMENT NEEDED
- Chopstick
- Gutter downpipe vertical mould
- Packaging tape

Time to complete: 1 day

Colours: I used only natural and two strengths of purple grass powder. A very light version gave me a light plum colour and a strong version gave me black.

Fragrance: 4 tsp (20 ml) black cherry fragrance.

METHOD
1. Cover the one side of the gutter downpipe with packaging tape.
2. Divide the batch – half for the plum, a quarter black and a quarter natural.
3. Pour the light plum into the mould, using it all – it should reach just over half of the mould.
4. Pour the natural, but only into one corner. You can lift the jug up high so that it penetrates deeply down the mould but still stays in one corner. Then do the same with the black.
5. Using a chopstick, draw lines from that same corner, radiating out. You can run the chopstick cross-ways through those lines in an arch shape to create a full spiderweb effect (see diagram on p. 168).

142

FEATHER SWIRL

Rating: Easy

EXTRA EQUIPMENT NEEDED
- Any mould
- Thin skewer stick
- Dividers

Time to complete: 1 day

Colours: I used white, natural, indigo at 2 tsp (10 ml) and charcoal at 3 tsp (15 ml).

Fragrance: 4 tsp (20 ml) rosemary essential oil.

METHOD
1. I used my fancy imported mould, but you can create divisions with cardboard inserts that are well measured, tight and secure to prevent leakage.
2. Position the dividers at unpredictable spacings – you're not creating stripes now, but a feather effect.
3. Divide batter equally among the four colours. Pour these colours randomly into the sections.
4. Gently remove the divisions, allowing the sections to merge.
5. Swirl a skewer stick from one corner of the mould to make a pattern (see diagram on p. 168).
6. Repeat pattern from the opposite direction.

LEAF

This technique comes from my friend Helen at Aroma Greens in Taiwan (service@soapmaker.com.tw).

Rating: Easy

EXTRA EQUIPMENT NEEDED
- Chopstick or knitting needle
- Loaf mould or individual moulds

Time to complete: 1 day

Colours: Natural and chromium oxide green.

Fragrance: 4 tsp (20 ml) rosemary essential oil.

METHOD
1. Keep half the batch neutral and colour the other half green with chromium oxide, well strained through muslin.
2. Fill half the mould with green.
3. Spoon the natural layer on top, taking care not to break though.
4. Then pour a small dot of green onto the natural layer in the middle of each mould (or, in a loaf pan, four or five dots along the length of the mould).
5. Either form your leaf now or pour a further dot of natural batter into the middle of the green dot to create a double leaf.
6. Now take your chopstick and move through the soap from corner to corner, crossing through the middle of the dot with a flared curve to the end (see diagram on p. 168).

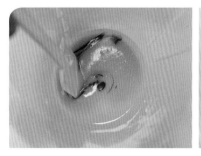 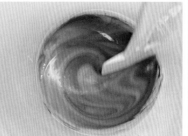 

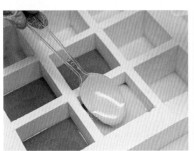

SUSPENDED BLOCKS

Rating: Moderate

EXTRA EQUIPMENT NEEDED
- Square individual moulds or a loaf pan
- Brick mould, so that slices from it will create squares

Time to complete: 2 days

Colours: I used all sorts of natural clays and a natural base.

Fragrance: 4 tsp (20 ml) sweet orange essential oil.

METHOD
1. Make a quarter batch of soap to pour the brick moulds with various colours of clay, or do this when you are doing another project as it will not use a lot of soap batter.
2. Harden overnight. Slice these bricks into square slices and pack these into pillars.
3. Lay them down in the mould, horizontally or vertically.
4. Pour natural batter to fill the moulds.
5. If you are using a loaf pan, you need to make your piles of squares long enough to be able to jam them between the ends of the mould so that they can be suspended in the centre of the soap.

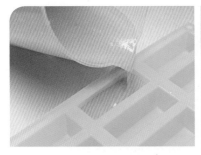

IN-THE-JUG SWIRL

Rating: Easy

EXTRA EQUIPMENT NEEDED
- Any individual silicone moulds will work, or gutter downpipes, or loaf pans. This technique can be used for many projects.

Time to complete: 1 day

Colours: Cocoa powder and natural.

Fragrance: 4 tsp (20 ml) coffee fragrance.

METHOD
1. Divide batter into two or more batches.
2. Colour the batches and then pour one jug into the next. Pour from a height so that the weight of the batter stream causes its own swirl.
3. Do not stir – simply pour.

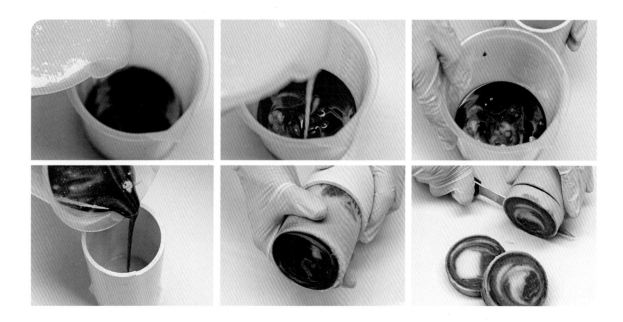

STRIPED BOX

Rating: Easy

EXTRA EQUIPMENT NEEDED

I found these moulds at a chocolate shop. They are intended to make little boxes for sweets or chocolates. This is not really a technique as such, just an interesting end soap that's produced using these unusual moulds.

Time to complete: 4 days

Colours: These require so little batter that I poured them over a few days using leftovers from other projects.

Fragrance: I did not add any further fragrance.

METHOD

I poured various layers down the sides to create the box, allowing each layer to harden overnight. Then the box was removed from the mould and the cavity was filled with a complementary colour to complete the soap block.

(5)

troubleshooting

Almost all problems result from inaccurate measuring. Soap making is a scientific chemical reaction and demands precision. I cannot stress enough how often you need to check your weights. Make sure you've zeroed your scale (to account for the container) using the tare button. If you get interrupted while measuring, start over. Don't take chances with measuring – it is crucial. Also make sure that your scale hasn't been dropped causing it to become inaccurate. Remember – soap ingredients are always weighed in mass and **not** calculated in volume.

some common problems

MY SOAP MIXTURE WON'T TRACE

- Perhaps you've given up too soon. If you are stirring with a whisk or wooden spoon, it can take 3–4 hours. With a stick blender, it should take no more than 5–20 minutes, depending on batch size and other factors.
- Your measurements may be incorrect – too little lye or too much water. Too much water and the soap will likely trace, but take extremely long to do so. Too little lye and you can't save the batch. It won't form soap.
- You're stirring too slowly. Stirring must be continuous and brisk.
- Your temperatures are not high enough – don't work below 95°F (35°C).
- Saponifcation is an exothermic reaction (it relies on heat that gathers as the reaction progresses), which means trace or saponification needs heat and movement (stirring) to take place.
- If you're making pure olive oil soaps, this is normal. They can take many hours to trace.

THE ADDITIVES FALL TO THE BOTTOM
You have added them too soon – at too thin a trace to be able to suspend them. Keep blending till you have a much thicker trace, then stir them up and they should suspend.

MY SOAP IS NOT FIRM – IT'S SOFT TO THE TOUCH
Your saponification process under-reacted, probably because there was not enough heat, or your lye measurement was wrong.

MY SOAP IS CRUMBLY, HARD AND BRITTLE
Your measurements were wrong or your combination of oils was wrong and out of balance between hard and soft oils. This soap won't be safe to use.

MY SOAP TRACED, BUT TURNED TO LIQUID IN THE MOULD
This means you had a false trace. Your temperature dropped too fast, allowing the fats to naturally solidify rather than saponify. Put the batch onto gentle heat and keep stirring till you get true trace – you may be able to save it.

MY SOAP HAS NO FRAGRANCE EVEN THOUGH I PUT A LOT INTO THE RECIPE
Sadly this is a normal challenge – finding fragrances or essential oils that can cope with the caustic reaction. Trial and error is your only solution other than upping the percentage, or trying the rebatching method. Citrus oils are particularly susceptible to this problem.

MY SOAP DEVELOPED A FINE, WHITE, POWDERY LAYER ON THE TOP WHILE STILL IN THE MOULD

A little bit of soda ash is fairly normal in large batches and is a mystery. It is not serious and can be sliced off. Placing a sheet of commercial-weight wax paper directly onto the soap batter surface (wax side down) when you mould the soap can help.

MY SOAP BATTER WENT THICK AND LUMPY IMMEDIATELY AFTER I ADDED MY FRAGRANCE

This is called seizing. Most perfumes are made with synthetic ingredients and these can often cause a batch to seize. Some essential oils, especially spicy ones, also cause batter to seize. If you work really fast and get your seizing batter into the moulds, the texture will even out during the gel phase and your batch won't be ruined.

MY SOAP BATTER WENT THICK AND LUMPY IN THE POT

Your temperature was too low or too high.

MY SOAP BATTER WENT STREAKY IN THE POT

Either your temperature wasn't hot enough, or this was caused by alcohol or dipropylene glycol in your fragrance. Mould it and it should turn out okay.

MY SOAP HAS A THICK LAYER OF CRUMBLY CRYSTALS ON THE SURFACE

Discard this soap. It is lye heavy and caustic and cannot be used.

MY SOAP HAS BEEN CURING, BUT IS GETTING FUNNY BROWNY ORANGE MARKS – LOOKS LIKE A DISEASE

You have DOS (dreaded orange spots), which is caused by unsaponified oil in the mixture turning rancid. This will smell bad and can be used on pets, but not for sale.

THE COLOUR OF MY SOAP CHANGES ALL THE TIME – IT KEEPS GETTING DARKER OR LIGHTER AS IT CURES

Darkening is usually caused by the chemical composition of essential oils or fragrances – especially the vanillin in vanilla, which tends to colour soap over time. Lightening is usually from using food-grade colourants that aren't stable and will fade.

THERE SEEM TO BE POCKETS OF LIQUID IN MY SOAPS WHEN I CUT THEM

This is unsafe soap as the lye mixture has not fully combined and will be caustic.

MY SOAPS START TO SMELL RANCID EVEN BEFORE THEIR CURE PERIOD IS OVER

The formulation has been superfatted and there are too many oil molecules for the lye to saponify. These pockets of unsaponified oil turn rancid over time, causing a bad odour. Oils with a very short shelf life, like hemp oil, are extremely prone to this.

6

packaging

I love beautiful packaging – I have a packaging board on Pinterest that is well worth looking at – search for RAIN.

Packaging is not just protection for your end product – it's a whole art on its own. First impressions count. They tell a story before you use the product. They tell you if it's natural, high-end, cheap and crafty, or exclusive. It sets the scene and provides a stage on which the product can perform. Attention to detail is important, especially if you plan to sell your soaps.

starting out

Packaging and label printing can be extremely costly. Your challenge is to make your own packaging without it looking as if it came from a bazaar. If you're at all artistic, you can design your own labels. If not, search the internet for free label templates. Many craft or food bloggers offer them as a perk to their blog followers. Join Pinterest and search there for free label templates you can download and print.

Boxes

Boxes elevate your soap to another level, making them that bit more exclusive and classifying them as a gift rather than for personal use. Some ideas for boxes are:

- Tins
- Plywood boxes in which you buy cheese – these come in round, oval or wedge-shaped. Try buying some from the cheese maker before they print on them.
- A pillow box is an easy option – templates can be found on the web.
- A foldable box and lid – templates are available online. Choose the paper carefully. The box and lid option can be made from old maps – these are strong and glossy and ideal for boxes. Or use the glossy pages of old magazines – choose pages with beautiful colours or pictures.
- Chinese takeaway boxes (plain ones) have such a pretty shape and can be dolled up to look really special. You may have to be creative about your soap shapes and sizes to make use of these as packaging.
- Cardboard tubes come in many diameters and can be a superb way of packaging soaps made in a round downpipe or Pringles mould.

You then need to decide whether your label will be stuck onto the box, or be a cigar wrap, or a swing tag tied around with ribbon or string.

Cigar wraps

This is a band of fairly thick paper that becomes your label and is wrapped around the centre of the soap. It works best with rectangular or long oval shapes.

Paper wraps

Search for interesting colours of wax paper to wrap soap as a gift. Other interesting packaging options are:

- Old maps
- Old dress patterns
- Used carbon paper
- Butcher's paper
- Gift wrap
- Magazine pages
- Yellowed pages from old books
- Sheet music

- Architectural plans and drawings
- Old handwritten letters or telegrams
- Pages from telephone books
- Newspapers – old ones
- Old photos (soak these to remove some of the backing by rubbing to make it thin enough to bend)

You can then opt for a sticker label or a swing tag.

Fabric pouches and bags

These can be easily made if you're vaguely able to sew. Alternatively, use fabric to wrap the soap in a kind of bundle. Look for handkerchief-sized pieces in sale bins, or simply buy handkerchiefs. Lacy ones work well. Read books on origami and find novel ideas on folding and making shapes, or look at books on entertaining to get ideas on how serviettes can be folded.

You can shred fabric into strips to create ties/ribbons. This would require a swing tag rather than a sticker label. Felt can be glued to make a soap pouch. It doesn't fray, so requires no stitching – a breeze for a non-sewer like me.

Packing on a soap dish or stand

Package your soap onto a soap dish or soap stand as a gift package. Always keep your eye open for bargains/sales on soap dishes.

Cupcake papers

A round soap could work well packaged in cupcake cups with a tie and label.

Knitted or crochet string pouches

This is a labour-intensive option, but if you use coarse string with an open crochet stitch, it won't take long to make a soap pouch that could double as a wash mitt.

Facecloths

Consider wrapping your soap in a facecloth as a gift presentation. Explore interesting ways of knotting the facecloth.

Leaves

I love the idea of packaging natural soaps in natural packaging. Leaves are wonderful if you have access to enough of the big leaves that would allow packaging – like banana leaves, elephant ears, tobacco leaves or the papery fibrous leaf from the mealie (maize).

Baskets

Like leaves, baskets make a superb natural packaging for a natural product. If you have cheap and easy access to them, use them. Nothing can beat natural fibres.

For more information on commercial packing and labelling requirements, go to our **website** (www.rainafrica.com).

glossary

Acid – low pH level

Alkaline – high pH level

Allergen – an ingredient that causes allergic reaction in certain individuals

Antibacterial – indicates an ingredient has the capability to fight bacteria

Antifungal – indicates an ingredient has the ability to inhibit growth of fungus

Antioxidant – an ingredient that helps prevent oxidation and oxygenation

Antiseptic – an ingredient that can prevent infection

Aromatherapy – using the power of inhaled fragrance on your brain's receptors to alter moods or promote mental wellbeing and relaxation

Batter – the traced cake-like soap mixture that is ready to mould

Caustic – highly alkaline in nature (high pH)

Certified organic – a natural material that has been officially checked, audited and certified by a certification body; this involves high cost and must be renewed annually

Cold process (CP) – a soap-making process whereby oils and fats are converted into soap without the addition of heat through cooking, by making use only of the latent heat from the melting of the fats and the natural heat generated by adding water and lye

Cure – the duration of 4–6 weeks that newly made soap takes to become mature, skin-friendly and a safe pH

D&C – Drug and Cosmetic, referring to colourants

Embeds – items you place in your soap when pouring – these could be other soap cut-outs or plastic toys (anything that can get wet)

Exfoliant – a slightly roughly textured powder from plants, herbs, spices, stone, seed or clay that helps to rub dry skin off the epidermis

FD&C – Food, Drug and Cosmetic, referring to colourants

False trace – when your soap batter's temperature falls below the melting point of any of the fats used, giving a false impression of trace when it has not traced, but begun to solidify

Gel phase – after trace, the soap batter, while being kept warm, has enough latent heat to begin to liquefy and then turn into a gel, becoming almost translucent. It is at this phase that translucent soap is made by adding alcohol and sugar to prevent the crystals from reforming into opacity.

Hand mill – when you grate down offcut soaps to re-constitute with heat and liquid

Hot process (HP) – a soap-making process that involves extra heat – cooking of the soap mixture to speed up the curing process and get the mixture to pH neutral without curing the soap for weeks. This is the technique used to make natural liquid soaps.

Humectant – an ingredient that attracts moisture from the air to itself, for example glycerine. In extremely humid weather, glycerine can be pulled to the surface of the soap by the moist air outside; this will then form into greasy little beads on the surface of the soap.

INCI name – an abbreviation for **International Nomenclature of Cosmetic Ingredients**. These are the globally recognised names of cosmetic ingredients that must appear on your labels if you sell soaps commercially.

Infusion – soaking plant material in boiling water to extract its properties, like tea

Lye – an intense alkali needed to make soap. In the old days it was obtained from soda ash – burning plantain skins, coconut husks or wood ash. In modern-day soap making, it is either sodium hydroxide (NaOH) or potassium hydroxide (KOH). The latter is used for liquid soap making.

Lye calculator – typically an Excel spreadsheet where the SAP values of oils are typed in to calculate the amount of lye needed to create soap with that particular combination of fats and oils

Lye solution – the mixture of lye and a liquid. So, when sodium hydroxide is added to water, it becomes a lye solution.

Organic – a natural material that has been grown without the use of any chemical pesticides or fertilisers and is not genetically modified

Oxidation – a process of which the result looks a bit like rust. The orange spots that are seen on soap caused by unsaponified oils turning rancid.

pH level – a scale of between 0 and 14 points, where 7 is neutral, below is acidic and above is alkaline

Potassium hydroxide (KOH) – the lye (alkali) material used for liquid soap making

Rancid – unsaponified oils or fats get exposed to air and turn smelly and stale, accompanied by orangey discoloration

Rebatching – the reprocessing of aesthetically failed soaps into slices, cubes, sticks or shapes to embed into an uncoloured soap batch for decorative effect

Saponification – the chemical process whereby fats and oils are converted into soap with the addition of lye, and consequently release glycerine

SAP value – abbreviation for saponification value, which means the amount of lye needed to convert an oil or fat into soap. This number is multiplied by the volume of the oil that you plan to use, to give you the amount of lye required to convert that oil into soap.

Seize – when a soap mixture starts to thicken and harden extremely quickly to a point where it becomes lumpy, cheese-like and unmanageable. Often caused by alcohol or certain perfumes with a high alcohol content.

Shelf life – how long something can last before going rancid or spoiling

Soda ash – a whitish powdery layer forming on the surface of soap indicating the interaction of lye with carbon dioxide in the air

Sodium hydroxide (NaOH) –the lye (alkali) material used to make solid soaps

Superfatting – adding extra fats and oils to the chemical process beyond what is minimally needed, to produce a richer, creamier, gentler bar. Normally only 5%. These fats remain unsaponified, so the soap is more prone to rancidity or the formation of orange spots, and will be a softer bar.

Tare function – this is a button on your scale where you can set the display window to read zero even if you have something on the scale. This means the scale is only weighing the contents of the container, not the container.

Trace – the critical point at which a soap mixture thickens enough to leave a little pathway across its surface when you dribble the liquid from the stick blender or spoon – as if a snail has walked along the mixture.

Tocopherols – soap preservative that comes from the vitamin E family

Unsaponifiables – fatty acids that don't convert to soap and remain in the same form in the finished bar

Vegan – a vegetarian who will also not use any product containing beeswax, honey, or dairy. Vegans will also only buy products with a traceability record to prove that no raw materials or the end products have been tested on animals.

saponification chart

	KOH	NaOH
Almond oil (sweet)	193	137
Aloe vera oil	191	135
Apricot kernel butter	136	97
Apricot kernel oil	191	135
Argan oil	188	134
Avocado oil	187	133
Baobab oil	202	143
Castor seed oil	180	128
Cocoa butter	193	137
Coconut oil (refined)	252	178
Corn/Maize oil (*Zea mays*)	191	136
Cottonseed oil	191	136
Evening primrose oil (*Denothera biennis*)	184	133
Flaxseed oil (*Linum usitatissimum*)	190	135
Grapeseed oil (Chardonnay)	183	130
Grapeseed oil (Riesling)	191	135
Hazelnut oil	192	130
Hempseed oil	192	135
Jojoba (*Simmondsia chinensis*)	91	65
Kalahari melon seed oil	189	135
Macadamia nut butter	186	132
Macadamia nut oil	194	138
Mafura butter	194	200

	KOH	NaOH
Mango butter	188	136
Mango oil	186	132
Marula oil	190	135
Mongongo nut oil/Manketti	195	139
Olive butter	124	134
Olive oil	198	138
Palm oil	197	141
Peach kernel oil	191	136
Peanut oil	192	136
Pecan oil	190	135
Pistachio nut oil	186	133
Poppyseed oil	194	138
Pumpkin seed oil	191	133
Rapeseed oil	175	124
Rice bean oil	184	130
Rosehip oil	190	135
Safflower oil	191	136
Sesame seed oil	190	134
Shea butter	179	128
Soybean oil	190	135
Sunflower seed oil	189	135
Vegetable shortening	192	137
Walnut oil	191	135
Wheatgerm oil	183	131

diagrams

TRICOLOUR (P. 98)
aerial view

LOOPING SWIRL (P. 141)
side view

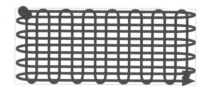

coat hanger

mould

BASIC SWIRL (P. 109)
aerial view

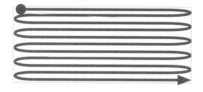

SPIDERWEB (P. 142)
aerial view

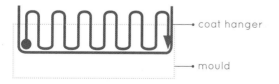

DIAGONAL SWIRL (P. 114)
aerial view

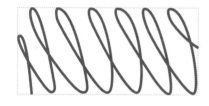

FEATHER SWIRL (P. 145)
aerial view

COAT-HANGER SWIRL (P. 138)
side view

coat hanger

mould

LEAF (P. 146)
aerial view

tip: I always hunt for interesting moulds in unusual shops like hardware stores, farmers' co-ops, plumbing suppliers, catering wholesalers or ship's chandlers. Interesting things are always where you least expect them to be!

tip: When it comes to moulds, ceramic and glass don't release the soaps, so stick to rubber, plastic, silicone, PVC and melamine.

where to find help

ONLINE HELP
First stop is www.rainafrica.com/tutorials – we have uploaded exciting video tutorials demonstrating basic soap-making skills, plus the techniques featured in this book and other exciting projects for you to try.

LYE CALCULATORS
www.soapcalc.com
www.cranberrylane.com/calculator.htm
www.thesage.com/calcs/lyecalc2.php
www.pinemeadows.net/lyecalc.php

HERB INFORMATION
www.botanical.com
www.margaretroberts.co.za

ESSENTIAL OILS INFORMATION
www.essentialoils.co.za

TEACHING SITES
www.teachshop.com
www.soapqueen.com (videos)

ONLINE FORUMS
www.soapmakingforum.com
www.soap-making-essentials.com

USEFUL SITES FOR SOAP BUSINESSES
Software and costing sheets
Calculators to upscale production
www.soapmaker.ca
www.colebrothers.com/soap

bibliography

The Soapmaker's Companion – **Susan Miller Cavitch** (published by Storey Books)
· For really superb technical explanations of the science and chemistry behind the saponification process.

Basic Soap Making – **Elizabeth Letcavage** (published by Stackpole Books)
· For really large, close-up, detailed photographs of the step-by-step soap-making process.

The Everything Soapmaking Book – **Alicia Grosso** (published by Adams Media)
· For great information on making your own recipes.

Soap Maker's Workshop – **Dr Robert S. and Katherine J. McDaniel** (published by Krause Publications)
· For a handy DVD and some very practical explanations about the chemistry aspects of soap making.

index

acknowledgements

It is such a privilege to be able to thank people publicly – it is my chance to voice my gratitude to others who have been angels along my path.

To my Heavenly God and Father who walks with me each step of the way, who has brought miracles in season, but has also brought challenges to make me grow in character and keep me on my knees. Thank you, my Lord.

My husband, George, who means everything to me – my soul mate, my onboard entertainment on life's uncertain journey. You have been at my side through the toughest of times and never stopped encouraging me. You have given me freedom to fly. Words cannot express the depth and width of my love and gratitude.

My mom, Carol, also fondly known as Cactus (not because she is prickly, but because she loves gardening). She is my safety net and my scaffolding. She cooks, shops, supervises the household and runs my life. Thank you, Marmie, SO much – everyone needs a mom like you.

My many precious, treasured friends who have endured my neglect over the years – if I start to name them, this list will be endless – you know who you are.

My RAIN family – every single one – who all contribute time and talent to make the brand what it is. Some of them have risen above deep and troubling personal tragedies, overcoming enormous life obstacles, to learn new skills and stretch themselves to new levels. They humble me and make me grateful for everything I have in life. Thank you for every contribution you make, both large and small.

My special work colleagues Malette and Annalena who have gone the whole nine yards with me. Through thick and very, very thin. Two more valuable allies you never could find. I am deeply indebted to you both. Annalena was responsible for the packaging section – dankie, dankie, dankie.

My business partners, Simon and Hendrien, who are the strength behind RAIN in the USA. Thank you for all the faith and trust you have shown in me.

Bruce, who took all the photos – I just LOVE working with you, Brucey Beans. You are going to be world famous one day.

Wilsia and the Metz Press team – thank you for the opportunity and for believing in me.

This edition published by Stackpole Books, 5067 Ritter Rd., Mechanicsburg, PA 17050

Library of Congress Cataloging-in-Publication Data
Missing, Bev, author.
  [Rain book of natural soapmaking]
  Soap making naturally / Bev Missing.
    pages cm
  Originally published Welgemoed, South Africa : Metz Press, 2014, under the title: The Rain book of natural soapmaking.
  Includes bibliographical references and index.
  ISBN 978-0-8117-1771-7
1. Soap. I. Title. II. Title: Soapmaking naturally.
  TP991.M57 2015
  668'.12--dc23

2015031349

First published in 2014
by Metz Press
1 Cameronians Avenue, Welgemoed
7530 South Africa

Copyright © Metz Press 2015
Text copyright © Bev Missing
Photographs copyright © Metz Press/
    Bruce Geils

PUBLISHER
Wilsia Metz
EDITOR
Thea Grobbelaar
PHOTOGRAPHER
Bruce Geils (Flyinghorse Photography)
DESIGNER
Liezl Maree
PROOFREADER
Estelle de Swardt
REPRODUCTION
Color/Fuzion, Green Point
PRINTED AND BOUND BY
PrintWORKS Global Services Pte, Ltd, China

ISBN 9780811717717